Encircling

the Christian Year

Published by
The Bible Reading Fellowship
15 The Chambers, Vineyard
Abingdon OX14 3FE
United Kingdom
Tel: +44 (0)1865 319700
Email: enquiries@brf.org.uk
Website: www.brf.org.uk
BRF is a Registered Charity

ISBN 978 0 85746 045 5

First published 2012
10 9 8 7 6 5 4 3 2 1 0
All rights reserved

Acknowledgments
Unless otherwise stated, scripture quotations are taken from the New Revised Standard
Version of the Bible, Anglicised Edition, copyright © 1989, 1995 by the Division of Christian
Education of the National Council of the Churches of Christ in the United States of America,
and are used by permission. All rights reserved.

Scripture quotations taken from the Revised Standard Version of the Bible are copyright ©
1946, 1952, 1971 by the Division of Christian Education of the National Council of the
Churches of Christ in the United States of America, and are used by permission. All rights
reserved.

Extracts from the Authorised Version of the Bible (The King James Bible), the rights in which
are vested in the Crown, are reproduced by permission of the Crown's Patentee, Cambridge
University Press.

Extracts from The Book of Common Prayer of 1662, the rights of which are vested in the
Crown in perpetuity within the United Kingdom, are reproduced by permission of Cambridge
University Press, Her Majesty's Printers.

Material taken from *The Treasures of Darkness* by Barbara Mosse is © Canterbury Press and is
used by permission of Hymns Ancient & Modern Ltd.

The paper used in the production of this publication was supplied by mills that source their
raw materials from sustainably managed forests. Soy-based inks were used in its printing and
the laminate film is biodegradable.

A catalogue record for this book is available from the British Library

Printed in Singapore by Craft Print International Ltd

Barbara Mosse

Encircling
the Christian Year

Liturgies and reflections
for the seasons of the Church

To Anthony,
with happy memories of RCM and
a shared ministry,
and for many years of deep friendship,
with love and gratitude

Acknowledgments

*Thanks to Martin for his patient and
insightful reading of the draft text, and to
Naomi Starkey for her encouragement
and enthusiasm for this project.*

*Thanks also to Jane Williams
for agreeing to write the foreword.*

Contents

Foreword

We have almost forgotten, in our day-to-day life, what it is like to live by patterns and rhythms that come not by choice but by the nature of the reality we live in. When we can buy any fruit and vegetables at any time of the year, irrespective of the season where we actually live; when we can regulate the temperature in our homes so that we can wear T-shirts in winter and fur in summer, then it is easy to lose touch with the grace of the patterns of life.

The Christian year re-embeds us in a bigger reality. As we follow the seasons of God's saving work, we rediscover that we are, as Genesis calls us, part of the generations of the heavens and the earth, part of the creative and transforming pattern of God's activity.

Barbara Mosse's book encourages us to take the time to find again a rhythm of life that becomes as natural as a heart-beat, as the rising of the sun, the waxing and waning of the moon, the dying and living of Jesus Christ. This rhythm helps us to remember who we are, through leading us back to rest in God our maker.

Jane Williams
St Mellitus College

Introduction

In her lovely book *The Deeper Centre*, Eva Heymann writes of the spiritual inspiration she receives from meditating on the cycle of the seasons. She marvels at the hidden strength which allows the fragile, early shoots of springtime to progress to full maturity, and the transformation into summer provides opportunities to give thanks for the growth that has taken place. Autumn glories in a rich feast of colour and beauty, and the dark, cold barrenness of winter belies the hidden potential for new growth already at work beneath the surface of the unyielding earth.

The seasons of the Church's year offer a parallel cycle to those of the natural world, gifting us with similar patterns and opportunities for spiritual life and growth. The keen watchfulness and anticipation of Advent, with its powerful symbolism of light and darkness, gives way to the explosion of joy that comes as we welcome the birth of Christ; the sombre penitential season of Lent leads us through the despair of the cross to the unimaginable wonder and joy of the resurrection. But our journey into God is far more than a succession of spiritual high points, and perhaps the weeks of Ordinary Time[1] encourage us to persist patiently in our walk with Christ during those times when nothing 'spectacular' seems to be happening.

Beginning with Advent Sunday, this book takes the form of a series of short liturgies consisting of an opening prayer, reading, reflection, bidding prayers and a closing Collect. The Collect has a long history as a special prayer for a given

Sunday that 'collects' or gathers up the biblical ideas and teaching for that week. This book offers a fresh set of Collects to complement the traditional ones and seeks similarly to reflect the week's teaching. One liturgy is provided for each week of the year and for the major festivals, and a complete cycle is offered for Holy Week. There are also a number of Red Letter days, listed separately after the main weekly sequence, which are limited to those saints and events most closely connected with the life of Christ. Given the complications of a three-year cycle of lectionary readings, I have chosen to range across the whole spectrum of services available for any given Sunday over the three years. Most readings come from the canonical scriptures of the Old and New Testaments, but I have also made occasional use of readings from the apocryphal Old Testament books of Wisdom and Ecclesiasticus, which are accepted as part of scripture by the Roman Catholic and Eastern Orthodox Churches.

It is hoped that this book may prove useful in a variety of ways. Although generally following the Sunday readings it can be used at any time, by either individuals or small groups. The brief and compact form of each piece may make it particularly helpful for those away from home—while in hospital perhaps, or on holiday, or travelling. Above all, these pieces offer an invitation to deeper prayer; to grow in our relationship with the God who loves us and accompanies us through all the seasons of our lives.

Advent

The long, dark night of history is almost over, and the promise of a new dawn lingers enticingly, just beyond the horizon of our sight. There have been false dawns and beguiling but mistaken paths along the way, but this time feels different. Now it is time to wake out of sleep ...

Advent Sunday

Opening prayer

Holy God, we thank you that you are a God who comes. This Advent-tide, sharpen our eagerness to hear your voice and deepen our desire to rest in your vibrant stillness. Like the watchmen of Israel, may we yearn for your dawning brightness; strengthen our hearts and enliven our spirits in joyful hope for the One who is to come. Amen

Reading

Besides this, you know what time it is, how it is now the moment for you to wake from sleep. For salvation is nearer to us now than when we became believers; the night is far gone, the day is near. Let us then lay aside the works of darkness and put on the armour of light; let us live honourably as in the day, not in revelling and drunkenness, not in debauchery and licentiousness, not in quarrelling and jealousy.

ROMANS 13:11–13

Reflection

Today the hallowed and mysterious time of Advent dawns, and the season's readings confront us with a sharp and increasing urgency. Wake up! *Now* is the time. 'Keep awake therefore, for you do not know on what day your Lord is coming' (Matthew 24:42).

For the Old Testament people, the long night of sleep was centuries old, and in their waking they were urged to be like watchmen on the city walls, straining their eyes for the coming dawn (Psalm 130:6). For the early Christians, the age-old pattern of watching and waiting gained fresh urgency in the dangerous years following Jesus' resurrection. With persecution rife and death an ever-present reality, Paul urged the Romans to wake up and 'live honourably as in the day' while eagerly waiting for the Lord's return.

Between these past and future Advents, a third invites us. In a few weeks' time we shall sing, 'O holy child of Bethlehem, descend to us, we pray; cast out our sin and enter in, *be born in us today*.' Without our openness to the coming of Christ in our hearts now, and our willingness to live in his light, Advent past is little more than nostalgic yearning, and hope for Advent future an impossible dream.

Short silence

Bidding prayers

Let us open our hearts in praise and thankfulness to the God who comes to us in every moment of our lives.

God of eternity, you spoke of old through the patriarchs and the prophets. Open our ears, Lord, to the prophetic voices in our world today:
Maranatha; come, Lord Jesus.

God of eternity, in love you come to us, offering forgiveness for sin and healing for our souls. May we become ever more aware of our need for you:
Maranatha; come, Lord Jesus.

God of eternity, you lovingly challenge us through the bracing call of your Spirit. May we be willing to cooperate with you in spreading the light of your kingdom:
Maranatha; come, Lord Jesus.

God of eternity, increase our watchfulness and strengthen our hope in the glorious reality of the coming dawn:
Maranatha; come, Lord Jesus.

Collect

Almighty Father,
all eternity resounds
with the vanguard of your coming Son.
In the company of all who have yearned for his coming
in ages past and those in ages yet to be,
may our hearts be glad and our spirits refreshed
as we wait in hope for the promised dawn.
For Jesus' sake we pray.
Amen

The Second Sunday of Advent

Opening prayer

Lord God, you come to us from all eternity with gifts of wisdom and love. May we worship you in awe and wonder, and may the prophetic voices of old find fresh resonance in our hearts, this Advent-time and always. Amen

Reading

A shoot shall come out from the stock of Jesse, and a branch shall grow out of his roots. The spirit of the Lord shall rest upon him, the spirit of wisdom and understanding, the spirit of counsel and might, the spirit of knowledge and the fear of the Lord. His delight shall be in the fear of the Lord. He shall not judge by what his eyes see, or decide by what his ears hear; but with righteousness he shall judge the poor, and decide with equity for the meek of the earth.

ISAIAH 11:1–4A (READ ALSO VV. 4B–10)

Reflection

When Adam's flesh and Adam's bone
Sits at Cair Paravel in throne,
The evil time will be over and done.

So goes the old prophecy in C.S. Lewis' *The Lion, the Witch and the Wardrobe*, in which the land of Narnia is held fast in the frozen grip of winter by the evil White Witch. There is a resonance here of the prophetic voice of Isaiah, echoing down to us through the corridors of history. So familiar are his words likely to be to us that we automatically hear them

13

as a foretelling of the coming of Christ. Indeed, that is what they are—articulating our deep desire for a society of equity, peace and justice—but the prophecy also related directly to the society of the writer's own time, expressing a longing for a new and ideal Davidic king who would right present wrongs and usher in a new reign of peace and prosperity.

And this is not all, for such a reign would also usher in the reign of God through all creation: a new order would be initiated, where predators and prey would happily coexist. Such harmony may be difficult to imagine but God calls us all to hope and trust and to work with him for the coming of his kingdom.

Short silence

Bidding prayers

Let us pray to God, the wisdom of the ages, who comes to us from beyond the boundaries of time and space.

Son of David, branch of Jesse: open our hearts to your reign of justice and gentle love:
Lord of the ages, deepen our thirst for the coming of your kingdom.

Son of David, branch of Jesse: guide the leaders of the nations with your spirit of knowledge and wisdom:
Lord of the ages, deepen our thirst for the coming of your kingdom.

Son of David, branch of Jesse: open our ears to the cries of the poor, and the need for justice in our society:
Lord of the ages, deepen our thirst for the coming of your kingdom.

Son of David, branch of Jesse: may we long for that day when all creation is healed and renewed, and the earth is full of the knowledge of the Lord:

Lord of the ages, deepen our thirst for the coming of your kingdom.

Collect

Almighty God,
in times of old you spoke through the prophets,
infusing their words with the hidden presence of the Christ to
come;
may our hearts be attuned to your prophetic voice today,
and may your gifts of grace and discernment
reveal to us the hidden Christ,
veiled within the darkness and light of our world.
In Jesus' name we pray.
Amen

The Third Sunday of Advent

Opening prayer

Almighty God, we pray that you would challenge our souls with the urgency of your call to repentance and humility. Awaken us with the bracing wind of your Spirit, so that we may come to know more fully the One who baptises with the Holy Spirit and with fire. Amen

Reading

When John heard in prison what the Messiah was doing, he sent word by his disciples and said to him, 'Are you the one who is to come, or are we to wait for another?' Jesus answered them, 'Go and tell John what you hear and see: the blind receive their sight, the lame walk, the lepers are cleansed, the deaf hear, the dead are raised, and the poor have good news brought to them. And blessed is anyone who takes no offence at me.'

MATTHEW 11:2–6

Reflection

The time is drawing near, and John the Baptist erupts on to the scene with a difficult but vital vocation. Just how difficult can be gleaned from a patchwork of Gospel references: from his calling before conception (Matthew 3:3; Luke 1:13) and his recognition of Jesus while still in the womb (Luke 1:41) to the apparent failure of his mission and political murder by Herod (Matthew 14:1–12).

Through it all, we hear the refrain, 'He must increase, but I must decrease' (John 3:30). John had to drain the cup of that reality to its dregs, dying without the confirmation of any visible success to crown his life's work. And, as today's text shows, the assurance that was given came to him only second-hand.

How content are we to 'decrease' in our service of Christ so that he may increase? How willing are we to pass the baton on at the time of God's choosing? Do we hold on beyond the demands of our calling, fearful of a loss of status and prestige? It is not, perhaps, unnatural to feel a glow of satisfaction when something we do is well received, but are we able to sit lightly to that and genuinely give the glory to God?

Short silence

Bidding prayers

Let us praise God, who sends his messengers before him to proclaim the way of his Son.

Your prophet John the Baptist was a witness to the truth. At whatever cost, may we be witnesses to your truth today.
Open our ears, Lord, and teach us to listen.

Your prophet John the Baptist was a burning and a shining light. Help us to share that light with all whom we meet.
Open our ears, Lord, and teach us to listen.

Your prophet John the Baptist experienced doubt and uncertainty. In our times of anxiety, help us, with him, to hear Jesus telling of the signs of his kingdom.
Open our ears, Lord, and teach us to listen.

Your prophet John the Baptist was faithful to the end. Help us to live the life of faith to its fullest, confident in the constant love of God through all our strengths and weaknesses, our fears and hopes.

Open our ears, Lord, and teach us to listen.

Collect

Almighty God,
from before his birth you set the Baptist apart
and called him to prepare the way of your Son.
Open our hearts to his message of repentance and humility,
and may we, with him,
proclaim the coming of Christ
with our whole being;
through Jesus Christ our Lord.
Amen

The Fourth Sunday of Advent

Opening prayer

Heavenly Father, we pray that you would have compassion on our weakness and vulnerability, our doubts and fearfulness. May we learn from the example of Mary that where you call, you also strengthen and equip. In Jesus' name we pray. Amen

Reading

Now the birth of Jesus the Messiah took place in this way. When his mother Mary had been engaged to Joseph, but before they lived together, she was found to be with child from the Holy Spirit. Her husband Joseph, being a righteous man and unwilling to expose her to public disgrace, planned to dismiss her quietly. But just when he had resolved to do this, an angel of the Lord appeared to him in a dream and said, 'Joseph, son of David, do not be afraid to take Mary as your wife, for the child conceived in her is from the Holy Spirit. She will bear a son, and you are to name him Jesus, for he will save his people from their sins.'

MATTHEW 1:18–21

Reflection

In the week approaching Christmas in 2010, the BBC broadcast an absorbing drama, *The Nativity*, presenting a powerful and imaginative interpretation inspired by the familiar biblical narratives. In the drama, Mary's explanation of her pregnancy is greeted by all with disbelief at best and, at worst, murderous hostility. In one of the most shocking scenes, Mary and her mother are surrounded by a hostile crowd in the marketplace, who begin to stone them. They are saved only by fleeing to the synagogue for sanctuary.

Although not biblical, the scene is entirely in keeping with a society that routinely stoned women for adultery. The cool, almost detached way in which Matthew records Joseph's reaction and subsequent dream can shield us from what must have been a frightening and dangerous reality for Mary. How were people to understand? There was no precedent for it.

Mary's response within this sequence of events poses a sharp challenge to the ways in which we may live our lives of faith. How much are we prepared to risk in our obedience to God? How 'safe' do we need to feel before we will step out in faith? Are we prepared to allow God to lead us into areas where we may be misunderstood and perhaps harshly misjudged—for the sake of his kingdom?

Short silence

Bidding prayers

We bring our prayers to our loving heavenly Father, who understands all our weakness and human frailty.

Jesus Christ, Saviour, we pray for your world; fractured and wounded, aching to hear the good news of your love.
When fearing the unknown, Lord: deepen our trust.

Jesus Christ, Saviour, we pray for your Church; fractured and wounded, yet entrusted with your message of peace.
When fearing the unknown, Lord: deepen our trust.

Jesus Christ, Saviour, we pray for our communities; fractured and wounded, yet called to work together for the good of all.
When fearing the unknown, Lord: deepen our trust.

Jesus Christ, Saviour, we pray for ourselves; fractured and wounded, yet called to be beacons of hope and light in the darkness.

When fearing the unknown, Lord: deepen our trust.

Collect

Heavenly Father,
you called Mary to be the mother of your Son,
with Joseph as her beloved husband and protector;
as she trusted you when all seemed lost,
so help us to put our faith in you
when all around is hostile and unbelieving.
For you are our Father,
and you will not leave us
to face our difficulties alone.
In Jesus' name we pray.
Amen

Christmas

The light shines in the darkness, and the wonder and
mystery of God-made-flesh emerges in our midst.
We welcome his coming with joy, but the familiar words
of much-loved Christmas carols do not contain him.
He is to be found not centre-stage before the eyes
of an admiring world but in the small and disregarded,
the humble, the 'little ones' of this world who know their
yearning need of him. 'And the Word became flesh
and lived among us ...'

Christmas Eve (Midnight)

Opening prayer

Heavenly Father, on this most holy night we worship before you in praise and thanksgiving; we bow before you in joy and gratitude at the wonder and mystery of your generous, self-giving love. Amen.

Reading

The people who walked in darkness have seen a great light; those who lived in a land of deep darkness—on them light has shined... For a child has been born for us, a son given to us; authority rests upon his shoulders; and he is named Wonderful Counsellor, Mighty God, Everlasting Father, Prince of Peace.

ISAIAH 9:2, 6

Reflection

On reading these words, full of hope, the musically inclined may find the joyous music of Handel's oratorio *Messiah* ringing in their ears. At this holy time, the waiting hours of darkness are finally over and we welcome the Christ-child in the brilliant light of a new dawn.

Again we wonder at the multi-level interpretations of prophetic scripture. Written in the eighth century BC to celebrate the birth of a specific Judean king, this text came to find resonance with the births of later kings too. And, of course, the words find their deepest and most richly textured meaning and fulfilment in the birth of Christ.

The prophet paints a scene of joyful celebration: people shout and sing in jubilation, as if in gratitude for a successful harvest. The time of war and suffering is over, and all look forward with hope and confidence to a time of lasting peace and security.

But in Christ, this time of glad celebration also brings a reminder that God's ways are not our ways. With the birth of Jesus we are encouraged to place our hopes for a just and peaceful world not in the might and power of any earthly ruler but in the weakness and vulnerability of a small baby.

Short silence

Bidding prayers

We give joyful thanks and praise for Christ, born this day as a human child.

On this most holy night, we worship with the shepherds as they hear the joyful news of Christ's birth.
Lord Jesus Christ, be born in us today.

On this most holy night, we pray that you would touch our hearts afresh with compassion for the poor, the vulnerable and the destitute, and those for whom Christmas is not a happy time.
Lord Jesus Christ, be born in us today.

On this most holy night, we pray for the town of Bethlehem and for a lasting peace for the troubled lands of the Middle East.
Lord Jesus Christ, be born in us today.

On this most holy night, we pray for our families and friends and for all those who are estranged from those they love. May this Christmas be a time when hurts are healed and broken relationships restored.
Lord Jesus Christ, be born in us today.

Collect

Eternal Trinity,
we celebrate the life of the Word made flesh.
Enlighten our hearts as we remember
the miracle of his coming to us,
the inspiration of his living among us,
the sacrifice of his dying for us;
that death itself may be vanquished
and all creation restored to the Father's heart of love.
We ask this in the name of Jesus Christ our Lord.
Amen

Christmas Day

Opening prayer

Gracious Father, we thank you for the precious gift of your Son. At this season of joyful celebration, open our hearts afresh to receive the love of Christ. For we too are your children, and in the power of your self-giving love and forgiveness we are born anew. Amen

Reading

In the beginning was the Word, and the Word was with God, and the Word was God. He was in the beginning with God. All things came into being through him, and without him not one thing came into being. What has come into being in him was life, and the life was the light of all people. The light shines in the darkness, and the darkness did not overcome it… And the Word became flesh and lived among us, and we have seen his glory, the glory as of a father's only son, full of grace and truth.

JOHN 1:1–5, 14

Reflection

From the fathomless depths of eternity, the Christ-child enters our world and takes his first steps on his journey to the cross. It is a coming shrouded in mystery and obscurity, not at all what many of those who had been looking and longing for his coming were expecting.

The watching and longing for his coming had been intense and centuries old. But the strong and the powerful, the religious leaders who assumed they were privy to the secrets of God, simply did not see it. Those who did recognise his coming were those whom the powerful and privileged held to be of no account: the poor and humble, the simple and trusting, those without preconceptions, those whose inner hearts and eyes were open to receive the Lord of life whenever and wherever he might make himself known.

What of our own longing and yearning? Today we worship the baby in the manger, but do we also expect to meet Christ every day, in the pain and joy that are part of the tapestry of every human life? Christ promises that he will never leave us or forsake us, and, if we trust him, nothing that happens will be able to put us beyond the reach of his loving embrace.

Short silence

Bidding prayers

Let us praise Christ, the eternal Son of God, whose coming in human flesh offers the gift of new life to all.

Longed for from of old, you promise us a richness and abundance of life beyond our wildest imagining.
Open our eyes, Lord, to the wonder of your birth.

Strength of the weak and powerless, you offer the gift of your healing love to all who acknowledge their inner poverty and helplessness.
Open our eyes, Lord, to the wonder of your birth.

Healer and life-giver, you pour your love on all who will receive you.
Open our eyes, Lord, to the wonder of your birth.

Lover of justice and peace, you challenge us to live our lives in cooperation with your loving purposes.
Open our eyes, Lord, to the wonder of your birth.

Collect

Lord Jesus Christ, Son of God from all eternity,
in poverty and weakness
you enter our world from beyond the boundaries of time.
With the seekers of old,
alert our hearts to the silent mystery of your coming;
sharpen our yearning for the fullness of your love
and give us eyes to see you, the Saviour of the world,
born in our flesh and common humanity.
For your name's sake we pray.
Amen

The First Sunday of Christmas

Opening prayer

Dear Lord and heavenly Father, we thank you for the gift and example of Jesus. Nurture, we pray, our growing sense of identity as your children, and enable us to fulfil our calling with courage, confidence and trust. We ask this in Jesus' name. Amen

Reading

Now every year his parents went to Jerusalem for the festival of the Passover. And when he was twelve years old, they went up as usual for the festival. When the festival was ended and they started to return, the boy Jesus stayed behind in Jerusalem, but his parents did not know it. Assuming that he was in the group of travellers, they went a day's journey. Then they started to look for him... When they did not find him, they returned to Jerusalem to search for him. After three days they found him in the temple, sitting among the teachers, listening to them and asking them questions. When his parents saw him... his mother said to him, 'Child, why have you treated us like this?' ... He said to them, 'Why were you searching for me? Did you not know that I must be in my Father's house?'

LUKE 2:41–49 (ABRIDGED)

Reflection

In her masterly work *The Story of Painting*, Sister Wendy Beckett draws our attention to an intriguing painting by the 14th-century Sienese artist, Simone Martini. He produced a striking painting on today's theme, entitled *Christ Dis-*

covered in the Temple. Wendy Beckett describes it as 'an extraordinary evocation of the generation gap'. Jesus and his mother face one another with glaring incomprehension; Mary's hand is raised in protest, and Jesus' arms are folded uncompromisingly across his body. Joseph's hand is on Jesus' shoulder, his face a mask of anger. The scene has a ring of truth and is one that the parents of any child on the cusp of adolescence would surely recognise.

In our awareness of Jesus' divinity, we can sometimes overlook the all-too-human element present here. As the Gospel writer states, Jesus was only twelve years old and therefore, in the eyes of the Law, still a child subject to his parents' authority. But his adolescent wrestlings raise questions that are relevant to each one of us. What defines my identity? Is it my relationship to God, or do other loyalties take priority? Is my faith in God peripheral to my life, or is it rather the central core around which all else takes shape?

Short silence

Bidding prayers

We bring our prayers in confidence and trust to our loving Father, who holds all our lives in the palm of his hand.

We pray for parents, and all those who bear loving responsibility for the young; may they know your strength and refreshment.
Loving Father, hear the cries of your children.

We pray for those who are striving to forge their own identity in life; may they know your encouragement and support.
Loving Father, hear the cries of your children.

We pray for those who do not know their roots; may they know your wisdom and loving embrace.
Loving Father, hear the cries of your children.

We pray for those who are confused about their life-direction; may they know your guidance and your belief in them.
Loving Father, hear the cries of your children.

Collect

Heavenly Father,
though a child still, and subject to his earthly parents,
Jesus wrestled with a growing sense of his identity as your Son.
Help us to follow his example
and learn from the pattern of his growing
what it means to be both fully human
and a child of God.
We ask this in Jesus' name.
Amen

The Second Sunday of Christmas

Opening prayer

Heavenly Father, we seek your guidance both in times of crisis and in the ordinary routines of our daily life. May we be alert to your prompting, not only in what is in front of our eyes but also in the mysterious world intimated in our dreams. Amen

Reading

Now after [the wise men] had left, an angel of the Lord appeared to Joseph in a dream and said, 'Get up, and take the child and his mother, and flee to Egypt, and remain there until I tell you; for Herod is about to search for the child, to destroy him.' Then Joseph got up, took the child and his mother by night, and went to Egypt, and remained there until the death of Herod. This was to fulfil what had been spoken by the Lord through the prophet, 'Out of Egypt I have called my son.'

MATTHEW 2:13–15

Reflection

Joseph here encounters the next stage of his crash-course in divine guidance, and all of it, according to Matthew, has been happening through his dreams. This dream-tradition has an ancient pedigree: an Old Testament Joseph was guided through dreams at critical stages of his life (Genesis 37—50), and part of God's gift to the prophet Daniel was that he 'had insight into all visions and dreams' (Daniel 1:17).

At each critical stage, our Joseph's actions are seen as being directed by God through the medium of a dream: the reassurance that it was right for him to take Mary as his wife despite her mysterious pregnancy (1:18–25); the incident recorded in today's reading; the direction to return from Egypt to Israel after Herod's death (2:19–21), followed by the further dream-instruction to move again to the safety of Galilee (v. 22).

Religion has been aware of the phenomenon for millennia but, psychologically speaking, the unconscious is a relatively recent discovery. Describing our conscious lives as being like the visible part of an iceberg, psychologists have likened the unconscious to the much larger part that is invisible below the water. We 'know' very little of what actually informs our conscious actions, and dreams are one of our main channels into the unconscious. Given careful attention, they can be a means of God's guidance and healing.

Short silence

Bidding prayers

We bring our prayers to God, who knows and loves us as we really are, and is aware of our needs before we ask.

Strengthen our sensitivity, Lord, to the subtlety of your creative presence in our conscious lives.
Speak to us, Lord, in the hidden mystery of our inner being.

Alert our ears, Lord, to the secret promptings of your Spirit in our unconscious lives.
Speak to us, Lord, in the hidden mystery of our inner being.

Deepen our awareness, Lord, of the ways in which the unconscious can influence our outer behaviour.
Speak to us, Lord, in the hidden mystery of our inner being.

Sharpen our appreciation, Lord, of the rich variety of the whole of our life and experience.

Speak to us, Lord, in the hidden mystery of our inner being.

Collect

Almighty God,
you spoke to our forebears through dreams and visions of the night,
bringing assurance of your presence,
warning of danger
and giving direction for the way ahead;
May we be open to your word in the sleeping hours of darkness
and alive to your presence with our dreaming self,
that, restored and refreshed,
we may with confidence greet the new day's dawn.
Through Jesus Christ our Lord.
Amen

FROM *THE TREASURES OF DARKNESS*, P. 57

Epiphany

So the light born in darkness and obscurity is announced to the world—but only to those who seek, and watch, and wait with patience. Wise men from distant countries, following the path of a mysterious star; the aged Simeon and Anna, wise and holy ones, watching and waiting for the coming of the Lord's Messiah. His light still dawns for those who seek, and watch, and wait with patience ...

The First Sunday of Epiphany (The Baptism of Christ)

Opening prayer

Heavenly Father, you welcome us as your children and call us to lives of faithful love and service. May we offer ourselves to you in willing obedience and submission, taking as our pattern and inspiration your Son, Jesus Christ our Lord. Amen

Reading

Then Jesus came from Galilee to John at the Jordan, to be baptised by him. John would have prevented him, saying, 'I need to be baptised by you, and do you come to me?' But Jesus answered him, 'Let it be so now; for it is proper for us in this way to fulfil all righteousness.' Then he consented. And when Jesus had been baptised, just as he came up from the water, suddenly the heavens were opened to him and he saw the Spirit of God descending like a dove and alighting on him. And a voice from heaven said, 'This is my Son, the Beloved, with whom I am well pleased.'

MATTHEW 3:13–17

Reflection

The baptism of Jesus by John has always puzzled commentators. Why was John's baptism of repentance necessary for Jesus, if he was indeed sinless? John seems to ask that question himself, but Jesus' answer ('it is proper for us in this way to fulfil all righteousness', v. 15) does not provide easy clarification, and the traditional meaning attributed to Jesus' baptism (that it publicly marked his identification with the human race) is not wholly explained by the enigmatic nature of his response to the Baptist.

For Matthew, Jesus' baptism is a hugely significant Christ-ological event, whose meaning is cryptically indicated in the words of the voice from heaven (v. 17). While directly affirming Jesus as the Son of God, they also hint that this role also involves that of the suffering servant (from the first Servant Song in Isaiah 42, later cited in its entirety in Matthew 12:18–21). To be the Son of God is to be also the suffering servant, and it points Jesus to a ministry of self-giving, sacrificial love. This is a theme that threads its way through all the Gospels and is pictured most graphically, perhaps, in the fourth Gospel. Here we find Jesus washing his disciples' feet (John 13:3–20) and urging his followers to imitate him in mutual obedience and loving submission.

Short silence

Bidding prayers

We bring our prayers to God in hope and trust, thankful that all things are possible to him.

God of living water, we pray for a world in crying need of your love and healing: may those with responsibility for leadership exercise their authority with wisdom and humility.
Lord, in your mercy, hear our prayer.

God of living water, we pray for all who come, or are brought, to baptism: may they come to know the mysterious working of God in their lives.
Lord, in your mercy, hear our prayer.

God of living water, we pray for all who serve in your name: may they recognise the Christ-light in all to whom they minister.

Lord, in your mercy, hear our prayer.

God of living water, strengthen and encourage our hearts with the gift of your abundant life: may we know that our weakness is made perfect in your strength.

Lord, in your mercy, hear our prayer.

Collect

Loving heavenly Father,
you drew your beloved Son to baptism by John in the river Jordan.
Through the gift of your living water
pour upon us the riches of your grace,
that we may know ourselves as your beloved children,
adopted in your love
and sent out with your compassion to serve a needy world.
Amen

The Second Sunday of Epiphany

Opening prayer

Heavenly Father, you call us to follow your Son with obedience and trust. Help us to listen to his voice with urgent attention, that we may follow him wherever he may lead. We ask this in Jesus' name. Amen

Reading

As [Jesus] walked by the Sea of Galilee, he saw two brothers, Simon, who is called Peter, and Andrew his brother, casting a net into the lake—for they were fishermen. And he said to them, 'Follow me, and I will make you fish for people.' Immediately they left their nets and followed him. As he went from there, he saw two other brothers, James son of Zebedee and his brother John, in the boat with their father Zebedee, mending their nets, and he called them. Immediately they left the boat and their father, and followed him.

MATTHEW 4:18–22

Reflection

In this starkly uncompromising passage, Jesus calls his first group of disciples. Spare in detail, it is blunt and unmistakable in its demand: 'Follow me.' In Matthew, these four men are fishermen who have no prior knowledge of Jesus and are usefully occupied in their work. They have seen no miracles and heard no teaching—nothing that would naturally lead them to leave work and family to follow a stranger.

Although it is not named as such, Matthew here records an early miracle, one where the powerful word of Christ is of itself sufficient to create a following. There are no blandishments or easy encouragements here, simply 'Follow me—now!' It was usual practice in this period for potential disciples to seek out the teacher, never the other way round, as here. But despite what they are leaving, the four respond immediately.

When later potential disciples hesitated, Jesus' response was blunt: 'Let the dead bury their own dead; but as for you, go and proclaim the kingdom of God' (Luke 9:60). In an age when it sometimes feels as if we are trying to induce people to come to church, how authoritative do we believe the word of Jesus to be? Have we the courage to allow it to speak for itself and to let it stand free of our own programmes and agendas?

Short silence

Bidding prayers

We bring our prayers to God, who loves us, calls us and equips us for his service.

Lord, you asked your disciples to leave what they knew for your sake.
Give us, we pray, the trust of those who know they are called to serve.

Lord, you asked your disciples to trust that obedience was the way of life and hope.
Give us, we pray, the humility of those who know they are called to serve.

Lord, you know our frailty and the fear that can keep us from whole-hearted response.
Give us, we pray, the confidence of those who know they are called to serve.

Lord, your words are the words of eternal life.
Give us, we pray, the peace and joy of those who know they are called to serve.

Collect

Almighty Father,
you called the disciples from work and family
to join you in the establishing of your kingdom.
When we hear your voice
yet are fearful of change,
give us the courage to offer our loving obedience
and to trust you
with all that lies ahead.
We ask this in Jesus' name.
Amen

The Third Sunday of Epiphany

Opening prayer

Heavenly Father, you call us to follow Christ and to spread the good news of your kingdom. We pray that, with Jesus, we may read the words of scripture and find them alive with the commission to serve you. We ask this in Jesus' name. Amen

Reading

When Jesus came to Nazareth, where he had been brought up, he went to the synagogue on the sabbath day, as was his custom. He stood up to read, and the scroll of the prophet Isaiah was given to him. He unrolled the scroll and found the place where it was written:

'The Spirit of the Lord is upon me, because he has anointed me to bring good news to the poor. He has sent me to proclaim release to the captives and recovery of sight to the blind, to let the oppressed go free, to proclaim the year of the Lord's favour.'

And he rolled up the scroll, gave it back to the attendant, and sat down. The eyes of all in the synagogue were fixed on him. Then he began to say to them, 'Today this scripture has been fulfilled in your hearing.'

LUKE 4:16–21

Reflection

The child Jesus has grown to manhood and he speaks in the synagogue as his unique mission beckons. There have been signs along the way: the words of the twelve-year-old child to his distressed parents, who thought him lost in Jerusalem,

44

'Did you not know that I must be in my Father's house?' (Luke 2:49b); the voice from heaven at his baptism, 'You are my Son, the Beloved; with you I am well pleased' (3:22b); his return from the temptations of the desert, empowered to teach and preach and heal (4:14). Now the scripture is fulfilled: 'The Spirit of the Lord is upon me, because he has anointed me to bring good news to the poor...'

With all this comes the dawning realisation that this mission is to cost not less than everything. We are called to share with Jesus in this mission, and the challenge it sets us is a stark one: 'No one who puts a hand to the plough and looks back is fit for the kingdom of God' (Luke 9:62).

Letting go of our hard-won securities is not easy, and we may not be offered instant reassurances. We are called to take the same leap of faith that was asked of the first disciples— to trust Jesus with all that we are, and to come to him with nothing but our naked desire and longing for God.

Short silence

Bidding prayers

We bring our prayers to Almighty God, who knows our strengths and weaknesses, our gifts and abilities.

Lord, you call us to preach good news to the poor.
May we know the anointing of your Holy Spirit.

Lord, you call us to proclaim release to the captives.
May we know the anointing of your Holy Spirit.

Lord, you call us to proclaim recovery of sight to the blind.
May we know the anointing of your Holy Spirit.

Lord, you call us to declare freedom for the oppressed.
May we know the anointing of your Holy Spirit.

Collect

Living Lord,
who, through your loving, longing and letting go,
discerned that you and your Father were one,
by your courage and example
enable us to respond fearlessly to the Father's love;
may we know him to be the fulfilment of our deepest desires,
where all that is most precious to us
finds its true place and perfection.
We make our prayer through you, our Lord and Saviour.
Amen

The Fourth Sunday of Epiphany

Opening prayer

Heavenly Father, we pray for a supple spirit, that we may be open to your compelling and creative word of love made visible in your Son, our Saviour Jesus Christ. Amen

Reading

They went to Capernaum; and when the sabbath came, he entered the synagogue and taught. They were astounded at his teaching, for he taught them as one having authority, and not as the scribes. Just then there was in their synagogue a man with an unclean spirit, and he cried out, 'What have you to do with us, Jesus of Nazareth? ... I know who you are, the Holy One of God.' But Jesus rebuked him, saying, 'Be silent, and come out of him!' And the unclean spirit, throwing him into convulsions and crying with a loud voice, came out of him... At once his fame began to spread throughout the surrounding region of Galilee.

MARK 1:21–28 (ABRIDGED)

Reflection

Another sabbath, another synagogue—and yet another facet of the authoritative word of Jesus is revealed. His right to stand up and teach in the synagogue was clearly recognised and accepted, and not only in his home town, but it very quickly became obvious that he was not just an ordinary teacher. The authority with which he taught 'astounded' his audience and quickly set him apart from the normal run of scribal teachers.

What further set him apart was his reaction to the man with an unclean spirit. There is a place for considering the ancient world's view of epilepsy or mental illness, but we wrong-foot ourselves if we get embroiled in such a discussion here. Whatever the nature of the man's actual illness, the point of the miracle is to demonstrate, yet again, the indisputable authority of the word of Jesus. We witness his authority in the miracle at Cana, in the call of the disciples, and as the transforming catalyst that turned round the life of the persecutor Saul.

These passages offer us part of a compelling, multi-faceted picture revealing the divine authority of Christ. It is perhaps worth asking again the question we considered a few weeks ago: in our own lives, how authoritative do we actually allow the word of Jesus to be?

Short silence

Bidding prayers

In hope and trust, we bring our prayers to God, who calls us to glad and willing response to the generosity of his love.

May our ears be open, Lord, to the challenging power of your word.
Heavenly Father, inspire us through the power of the Word made flesh.

May our minds be open, Lord, to the healing power of your word.
Heavenly Father, inspire us through the power of the Word made flesh.

May our hearts be open, Lord, to the enlivening power of your word.

Heavenly Father, inspire us through the power of the Word made flesh.

May our lives be open, Lord, to the transforming power of your word.

Heavenly Father, inspire us through the power of the Word made flesh.

Collect

Lord Jesus Christ,
you speak the word of life
to rebuke, console, command and heal.
Sharpen our ears
to the urgency of your word,
and compel us through your love
to respond with obedience and trust.
We ask this in your name, and for your sake.
Amen

Ordinary Time
before Lent

The first mighty wave in the drama of the incarnation
has been accomplished. We are invited to pause briefly
to catch our breath and consider the words of some
of those who have glimpsed the vision of Christ's light
abroad in the world. As we reach the threshold of Lent,
we stand with Elijah on the mountain-top, our spiritual ears
intent on hearing the Lord in 'a sound of sheer silence'.

The Fifth Sunday before Lent

Opening prayer

Heavenly Father, we thank you that you proclaim the mystery of your redeeming love in the generous self-giving of a crucified Saviour. Help us so to walk in the steps of Christ that we may see in him alone the means of grace and the hope of glory. Amen

Reading

I did not come proclaiming the mystery of God to you in lofty words or wisdom. For I decided to know nothing among you except Jesus Christ, and him crucified... My speech and my proclamation were not with plausible words of wisdom, but with a demonstration of the Spirit and of power, so that your faith might rest not on human wisdom but on the power of God... But we speak God's wisdom, secret and hidden, which God decreed before the ages for our glory. None of the rulers of this age understood this; for if they had, they would not have crucified the Lord of glory.

1 CORINTHIANS 2:1–8 (ABRIDGED)

Reflection

These words of Paul to the troubled Corinthian church are heartfelt and urgent, and they speak to us across the centuries with clarity and conviction. Paul makes a compelling plea to a body of Christians who are tearing themselves apart through factions and quarrels—a situation that is, tragically, not unknown to us in the Church of today.

This division is not, and never has been, the way of Christ. One of the most startling indications of the precise nature of the mysterious power of God in Christ comes in John's Gospel: 'Jesus, knowing that the Father had given all things into his hands… poured water into a basin and began to wash the disciples' feet' (13:3, 5). Our human minds wrestle with the paradox: Jesus, who knows that his Father has given him all things, demonstrates his authority by washing the feet of his disciples.

This is the model for Christian discipleship that Jesus sets before us, and Paul points his readers to the mysterious reality of the paradox it contains. Have nothing to do with factions, and resist the temptation to dominate by trying to shout the loudest. Walk rather with Jesus in the way of the cross, humbly seeking the hidden wisdom of God, which is revealed only in perfect humility and self-forgetful love.

Short silence

Bidding prayers

With humility and confidence we bring our prayers to almighty God, in whom we discover the secret wisdom of eternity.

We pray for the rulers of the nations, that they may serve their people with humility and compassion.
Jesus Christ, Lord of glory, lead us in the way of your cross.

We pray for the leaders of the Church, that they may set before God's people the servant-leadership of Christ.
Jesus Christ, Lord of glory, lead us in the way of your cross.

We pray for those who work tirelessly for the good of others, that they may look to God and draw their strength from his secret wisdom.
Jesus Christ, Lord of glory, lead us in the way of your cross.

We pray for ourselves, that in our lives and relationships we may know nothing but Christ, and him crucified.
Jesus Christ, Lord of glory, lead us in the way of your cross.

Collect

Almighty God,
with you is wisdom, secret and hidden
since before the birth of time and space.
Clarify our vision, so that we may see in the cross
the glory of Christ,
and that in him we may come to know
the strength that is made perfect in weakness,
and the power that alone can conquer death.
We ask this in Jesus' name.
Amen

The Fourth Sunday before Lent

Opening prayer

Heavenly Father, may our relationships with others this day be exercised in a spirit of love and humility. When we are wronged, make us eager to forgive, and when we have wronged others, may we be quick to seek forgiveness. We ask this in Jesus' name. Amen

Reading

'You have heard that it was said to those of ancient times, "You shall not murder"; and "whoever murders shall be liable to judgment." But I say to you that if you are angry with a brother or sister, you will be liable to judgment; and if you insult a brother or sister, you will be liable to the council; and if you say, "You fool", you will be liable to the hell of fire. So when you are offering your gift at the altar, if you remember that your brother or sister has something against you... first be reconciled... and then come and offer your gift.'

MATTHEW 5:21–24 (ABRIDGED)

Reflection

'Do not think that I have come to abolish the law or the prophets; I have not come to abolish but to fulfil.' So states Jesus, a few verses before the opening of today's passage (v. 17). Now, using practical and down-to-earth examples, he begins to explain just what this must mean for his followers. Taking aspects of human sin dealt with under the Hebrew law (murder and, later, adultery and false witness), Jesus takes the law's teaching to new depths. Obedience to the

55

literal meaning of the commandments is no longer enough: there are many ways in which we can 'kill' others through our resentment and lack of love, and Jesus is adamant that anger and hostility can have no place in God's kingdom.

A counsel of perfection, we may think. But such falling from grace is a natural consequence of human sin, and, when such instances occur, Jesus states clearly how we should respond. 'If you remember that your brother or sister has something against you, leave your gift there before the altar and go; first be reconciled…' (vv. 23b–24a). The remedy that Jesus offers is simple but far from easy. It requires of us courage, humility and self-knowledge, a willingness to make the first move, and a refusal to cling to angry self-righteousness, however much we may feel it is justified.

Short silence

Bidding prayers

Let us bring our prayers with confidence to our heavenly Father, in whose forgiving love we are called to live in peace with one another.

Abba, Father, help us to live peaceably as members of your creation, knowing that we are loved and forgiven.
Lord, forgive us our sins; as we forgive those who sin against us.

Abba, Father, help us to live peaceably as members of the human family, knowing that we are loved and forgiven.
Lord, forgive us our sins; as we forgive those who sin against us.

Abba, Father, help us to live peaceably as members of our families and local communities, knowing that we are loved and forgiven.
Lord, forgive us our sins; as we forgive those who sin against us.

Abba Father, help us to live peaceably with ourselves, knowing that we are loved and forgiven.
Lord, forgive us our sins; as we forgive those who sin against us.

Collect

Almighty God,
you call us as members of a living fellowship
to live in peace and harmony with one another.
Forgive us our weakness and failures,
our bitterness and petty resentments;
help us to forgive,
and grant us the humility
to reach out to those we have wronged
in penitence and love.
In Jesus' name we pray.
Amen

The Third Sunday before Lent

Opening prayer

Almighty Father, with you nothing is impossible. When we have been hurt, open our hearts to your transforming power, that we may know you more deeply as the source of all healing and peace. Amen

Reading

'You have heard that it was said, "An eye for an eye and a tooth for a tooth." But I say to you, do not resist an evildoer. But if anyone strikes you on the right cheek, turn the other also; and if anyone wants to sue you and take your coat, give your cloak as well… You have heard that it was said, "You shall love your neighbour and hate your enemy." But I say to you, love your enemies and pray for those who persecute you… For if you love those who love you, what reward do you have? Do not even the tax collectors do the same? … Be perfect, therefore, as your heavenly Father is perfect.'

MATTHEW 5:38–48 (ABRIDGED)

Reflection

Jesus continues to urge his hearers to move beyond the letter of the law. The saying, 'An eye for an eye and a tooth for a tooth' (originally a plea for proportionate punishment rather than excessive vengeance) is taken by Jesus to further challenging depths. Rather than striking out in retaliation, Jesus proposes a path of non-resistance and 'turning the other cheek'.

But even this, says Jesus, is not enough for the disciple. 'The other cheek' must not be turned in order to shame the offender or bring them further discomfort; actions are meaningless if the heart itself remains untransformed. Humanly, we may find it impossible to love our enemies; but these sayings nevertheless express the reality of life in God's kingdom. Lived to their fullest extent by Christ, they provide the only authentic pattern for the Christian disciple.

In 1947, the Dutch holocaust survivor Corrie Ten Boom was approached by a prison guard who had been one of those working at Ravensbrück concentration camp, where her sister had died. Holding out his hand, he asked for forgiveness. Almost overcome by her anger and repugnance, she describes a miraculous transformation: 'For a long moment we grasped each other's hands, the former guard and the former prisoner. I had never known God's love so intensely as I did then.'[2]

Short silence

Bidding prayers

We bring our prayers before our heavenly Father, seeking his love and forgiveness for the evils we see in the world and within ourselves.

We pray for the compassion and honesty to see the world as it is, with all its variegated facets of beauty and torment. Show us our weakness, and enable us to forgive.
Empower us, Lord, in your way of love and forgiveness.

We pray for the compassion and honesty to see our Church as it is, with all its variegated facets of holiness and humanity. Show us our weakness, and enable us to forgive.
Empower us, Lord, in your way of love and forgiveness.

We pray for the compassion and honesty to see our local communities as they are, with all their variegated facets of self-giving and self-living. Show us our weakness, and enable us to forgive.

Empower us, Lord, in your way of love and forgiveness.

We pray for the compassion and honesty to see ourselves as we really are, with all our variegated facets of light and shadow. Show us our weakness, and help us to forgive.

Empower us, Lord, in your way of love and forgiveness.

Collect

Lord Jesus Christ,
you call us to forgive the sins of others
and to pray for our persecutors.
Take our hand and lead us, we pray,
that our fear may be melted
and our bitterness swallowed up
in the miracle of your transforming love.
We ask this in your name.
Amen

The Second Sunday before Lent

Opening prayer

Almighty God, may our eyes be open to the light of your creative word, that in you our lives may find their true meaning and purpose. We ask this in Jesus' name. Amen

Reading

In the beginning when God created the heavens and the earth, the earth was a formless void and darkness covered the face of the deep, while a wind from God swept over the face of the waters. Then God said, 'Let there be light'; and there was light. And God saw that the light was good; and God separated the light from the darkness. God called the light Day, and the darkness he called Night. And there was evening and there was morning, the first day.

GENESIS 1:1–5

Reflection

Anyone who has seen Benjamin Britten's opera *Noye's Fludde* will remember the strident orchestral cacophony that builds to a climax as the flood reaches its height. Then, just when it seems impossible that the conductor could retain any control, the words of the hymn 'Eternal Father, strong to save' miraculously emerge from the musical mayhem. It is a supremely moving moment, somehow connecting with our deepest hope and belief that God is bringing and will continue to bring order out of the chaos of our inner and outer worlds.

In the opening of Genesis, we witness the very beginning of this timeless orchestration, when the creative word of God summons light out of darkness. That work of creation is continuing still—relentlessly, patiently, lovingly propelling all living things from darkness towards the light spoken forth by God. But this light is mysterious: it cannot be visible light, as the sun, moon and stars do not appear until the fourth day of creation. The ninth-century Celtic theologian Eriugena called it 'first light', emanating from the life and energy of the Godhead itself, invisible to our human sight but giving life to all created things. In the words of a familiar traditional hymn, 'Immortal, invisible, God only wise; in light inaccessible, hid from our eyes.'[3]

Short silence

Bidding prayers

We bring our prayers to God, seeking the creative power of his 'first light' in our lives and the life of the world.

For those whose world is ruled by injustice and fear, and who see no possibility of change.
Speak, Lord, in the darkness: let there be light.

For those whose world is ruled by poverty and hunger, and who have no means to feed themselves or their children.
Speak, Lord, in the darkness: let there be light.

For those whose world is ruled by a sense of right and entitle-ment, and who see no need to concern themselves with the sufferings of others.
Speak, Lord, in the darkness: let there be light.

For those whose world is ruled by a compelling need to work for peace and justice, and who find themselves striving against the powers of darkness.

Speak, Lord, in the darkness: let there be light.

Collect

God the Holy Spirit,
you brood over the seething potential of our inner chaos
with the brightness of your wings.
Transform our harsh dissonance
into music for your glory,
that we may live in your presence
created, redeemed and renewed;
through Jesus Christ our Lord.
Amen

FROM *THE TREASURES OF DARKNESS*, P. 41

The Sunday Next before Lent

Opening prayer

Almighty God, you speak to us in word and silence. May our hearts and spirits be attuned to your presence, wherever and however you may make yourself known to us. We ask this in Jesus' name. Amen

Reading

Then the word of the Lord came to [Elijah], saying, 'What are you doing here, Elijah? … Go out and stand on the mountain before the Lord, for the Lord is about to pass by.' Now there was a great wind, so strong that it was splitting mountains and breaking rocks in pieces before the Lord, but the Lord was not in the wind; and after the wind an earthquake, but the Lord was not in the earthquake; and after the earthquake a fire, but the Lord was not in the fire; and after the fire a sound of sheer silence. When Elijah heard it, he wrapped his face in his mantle and went out and stood at the entrance to the cave.

1 KINGS 19:9–13 (ABRIDGED)

Reflection

Last week, God spoke—and there was light. Today we witness a very different theophany: God's presence in silence. Exhausted and disheartened, Elijah has fled in fear for his life from the threats of Jezebel. On Mount Horeb, he witnesses a sequence of dramatic events—wind, earthquake and fire— but experiences God in none of them. Paradoxically, it is in the calm after the storm, in the mind-bending 'sound of sheer silence' (or 'still, small voice', KJV), that Elijah finally knows he is in the presence of God. He covers his face with his mantle, acknowledging that he is on holy ground (see Exodus 3:6).

Discipleship is far more than an outward calling that requires us to be active most of the time. We forget that all our activity needs to be nourished from a deep well of silence, where we find the secret guiding presence of God in the depths of the heart. Without that nourishment, we, like Elijah, will experience 'burn-out' and be unable to continue in our own strength. One of the things Elijah was able to learn in the silence was the ability to literally 'pass on his mantle'—symbolising his prophetic work—to Elisha. In the silence, we too are enabled to 'let go' and to learn the healing truth about ourselves and our place in the life of God's creation.

Short silence

Bidding prayers

Let us come before God in humility and thankfulness, seeking his love and his presence in the silent depths of our hearts.

When we are exhausted and frightened, and do not know which way to turn;
Speak through the heats of our desire, O still small voice of calm.

When we are discouraged by failure, afraid of getting up and trying again;
Speak through the heats of our desire, O still small voice of calm.

When we are confident, over-sure of our abilities, relying on ourselves rather than you;
Speak through the heats of our desire, O still small voice of calm.

When we hold on to things beyond their time because we are afraid that, if we let go, there will be nothing to replace them;
Speak through the heats of our desire, O still small voice of calm.

Collect

Mysterious God,
whose silence speaks louder than our words
and whose darkness guides more surely than our light,
may we trust you in cloud and in sunlight,
in the interplay of Word and Silence,
until we know as we are fully known.
Through Jesus Christ our Lord.
Amen

FROM *THE TREASURES OF DARKNESS*, P. 102

Lent

The atmosphere changes again, and the air becomes more bracing. Imperceptibly at first, the pace begins to quicken and our attention is sharpened. As Act 2 of the drama gets underway, we are again urged to be alert and awake, but this time the mood is keener, sharper. Beware of pride and complacency, for a time of great testing is approaching. The question faces us as it faced Jesus, 'Whom will you serve—God or Satan?' As the journey towards Jerusalem begins, there is no other choice.

Ash Wednesday

Opening prayer

Heavenly Father, we come before you in penitence and faith. Transform our self-centredness, so that we may live, pray and work, not for earthly reward, but with our hearts and wills focused on your kingdom. In Jesus' name we pray. Amen.

Reading

[Jesus said], 'Beware of practising your piety before others in order to be seen by them; for then you have no reward from your Father in heaven… When you give alms, do not let your left hand know what your right hand is doing, so that your alms may be done in secret; and your Father who sees in secret will reward you… And whenever you fast, do not look dismal, like the hypocrites, for they disfigure their faces so as to show others that they are fasting. Truly I tell you, they have received their reward.'

MATTHEW 6:1–4, 16 (ABRIDGED)

Reflection

The season of Lent begins with Ash Wednesday, which, from around the ninth century, has been marked in our churches by a service of general penance. Usually in the setting of a Eucharist, the foreheads of clergy and people are signed with a cross in ash, so setting a penitential tone for the whole season.

And yet, our penance, our giving, our fasting—all our good intentions and attempts to grow in humility—so easily turn to pride and self-serving. I remember with some discomfort the times when, as a young woman, I would come from an Ash Wednesday service wearing my ashen cross as some kind of badge of honour. Jesus knew this weakness in our nature only too well, and was quick to warn against it.

Be careful, he says, that your penance, your giving and your fasting are offered for the right reasons. They should be offered to God alone, not used as vehicles for your own pride and self-promotion. Those who are seeking the praise and admiration of others already have their reward. This is easier said than done, and, being human, our motives will always be mixed; yet we should strive to work in secret, so that the things we do for the sake of God and his kingdom are known to him alone.

Short silence

Bidding prayers

We come to God with soiled hands but with trust and hope in our hearts, seeking his cleansing and forgiveness.

Forgive us, Father, for the times when we have sought the admiration and praise of people rather than the reward of heaven.
Breathe on us, Lord, with the clean air of your kingdom.

Forgive us, Father, for the times when we have put our own interests before the needs of others.
Breathe on us, Lord, with the clean air of your kingdom.

Forgive us, Father, for the times when we have been so absorbed by the world that we have failed to hear your voice.
Breathe on us, Lord, with the clean air of your kingdom.

Forgive us, Father, for the times when we have trusted in our own ability, forgetting that everything we have comes from you.

Breathe on us, Lord, with the clean air of your kingdom.

Collect

Heavenly Father,
we seek to worship you with pure hearts,
yet so often find our motives mixed.
Inspire us by your Spirit, that we may breathe afresh
the clean air of your kingdom;
purify our hearts, that we may worship you
in spirit and in truth.
In Jesus' name we pray.
Amen

The First Sunday of Lent

Opening prayer

Almighty God, so often we fail to do the good we want to do, and do that which we should not. Strengthen us that we may resist temptation and forgive us when we fall, secure in the presence of Christ to encourage and uphold us. Amen

Reading

Then Jesus was led up by the Spirit into the wilderness to be tempted by the devil. He fasted for forty days and forty nights, and afterwards he was famished. The tempter came and said to him, 'If you are the Son of God, command these stones to become loaves of bread.' But he answered, 'It is written, "One does not live by bread alone, but by every word that comes from the mouth of God."' Then the devil took him to the holy city and placed him on the pinnacle of the temple... Again, the devil took him to a very high mountain and showed him all the kingdoms of the world... Jesus said to him, 'Away with you, Satan! For it is written, "Worship the Lord your God, and serve only him."'

MATTHEW 4:1–5, 8–10 (ABRIDGED)

Reflection

As the early church community struggled to articulate what it believed about the nature of Christ, a tendency developed (called 'Docetism', from the Greek *dokeo*, 'I seem') in which the general humanity and sufferings of the earthly Christ were thought to be only apparent, not real. The Docetists believed that the agonies Christ suffered through his passion and crucifixion were illusions, and, in the same way, his temptations in the wilderness were not real temptations at all.

A temptation can only be such if it hooks into a real tendency in our character, and the Gospel accounts of Jesus' experience bring the compelling and universal nature of these temptations into sharp focus. All of us tend to try to cut short a time of necessary testing in an attempt to relieve our discomfort; we all know the longing for power and control and the temptation to court public admiration by 'showing off'. Jesus shared these temptations with us all, and the fact that he successfully resisted them should be a source of endless hope and encouragement.

Jesus is one who 'in every respect has been tempted as we are, yet without sin' (Hebrews 4:15, RSV). A Christ who is only human or only divine can never fulfil our deepest need. We need to strive to hold both realities in equal tension and continue to wrestle with the mystery.

Short silence

Bidding prayers

We bring our prayers to God, who equips us to resist evil and lifts us up when we fall.

Lord, there are times when we reach for the easiest and most comfortable solution; but it is your way of trust that is balm for our souls.
In times of temptation, Lord, deliver us from evil.

Lord, there are times when we use power and control to conceal our insecurity; but it is your way of obedience that is balm for our souls.
In times of temptation, Lord, deliver us from evil.

Lord, there are times when we parade our abilities, seeking the admiration of others; but it is your way of humility that is balm for our souls.
In times of temptation, Lord, deliver us from evil.

Lord, in peace and security, trial and testing, we seek your guiding presence; but it is your way of love that is balm for our souls.
In times of temptation, Lord, deliver us from evil.

Collect

Gracious heavenly Father,
you know the areas of our frailty
and the temptations of our wilderness;.
in times of testing
when our will is weak,
may we be strengthened by your Spirit within
and encouraged by the presence and example
of Jesus Christ our Lord.
Amen

The Second Sunday of Lent

Opening prayer

Heavenly Father, we thank you that you are the God of new beginnings, and that your mercies are new every morning. Keep us, we pray, within the circle of your loving arms; forgive us our petty jealousies and strivings, and curb our restless wanderings so that we may find our true and eternal home in you. Amen

Reading

[Jacob] came to a certain place and stayed there for the night... Taking one of the stones of the place, he put it under his head and lay down in that place. And he dreamed that there was a ladder set up on the earth, the top of it reaching to heaven; and the angels of God were ascending and descending on it. And the Lord stood beside him and said, 'I am the Lord, the God of Abraham your father and the God of Isaac... Know that I am with you and will keep you wherever you go... for I will not leave you until I have done what I have promised you.' Then Jacob woke from his sleep and said, 'Surely the Lord is in this place—and I did not know it!' And he was afraid, and said, 'How awesome is this place! This is none other than the house of God, and this is the gate of heaven.'

GENESIS 28:11–13, 15–17 (ABRIDGED)

Reflection

An exile on the face of the earth, Jacob had left behind a troubled past, having stolen his brother's birthright. Weary, bruised and besmirched by sin, he is seeking... what? 'The

74

place of his resurrection', as the Celts called it? Stopping for the night and falling asleep, he dreams of a ladder stretching between earth and heaven, with angels ascending and descending upon it; and he hears the Lord speaking to him: 'Know that I am with you and will keep you wherever you go…' Jacob is awestruck. 'Surely,' he says, 'the Lord is in this place, and I did not know it.'

Like Jacob, we too may feel we are running from our past, the wrong we have done and all that has hurt us. We too are often weary, fearful and sin-soiled, and seeking… what? 'The place of our resurrection'? Then, miraculously, it dawns on us that wherever we journey, and whatever the weight of our sin and pain, *here* is 'the place of our resurrection'. If we come to God with open hearts and listen to his still, small voice, we will find that he is with us, offering forgiveness for our sin, healing for our wounds and peace for our troubled souls.

Short silence

Bidding prayers

In penitence and faith we come before our loving heavenly Father, seeking his healing and peace.

For the pilgrim Church on earth; that through all its divisions and perplexity it may yet be aware of the hidden glory of God in its midst:
Lord of our journey, show us your glory.

For all people of good heart, in their striving to make the world a better place; that they may become aware of the hidden glory of God in their midst:
Lord of our journey, show us your glory.

For people of troubled mind, seeking to flee the pain and sin of their past; that they may become aware of the hidden glory of God in their midst:
Lord of our journey, show us your glory.

For ourselves as we travel; that we may trust our Lord with our past, present and future, and that we may be aware of the hidden glory of God in our midst:
Lord of our journey, show us your glory.

Collect

O God of our journey and our resting places,
with you is healing and peace.
You were with us at the beginning;
you are with us now;
you will be with us for ever.
With the ebbing of the tide,
with the turning of the season,
grant us healing, forgiveness and peace.
O God of our journey and our resting places,
hear our prayer for Jesus' sake.
Amen

The Third Sunday of Lent

Opening prayer

Heavenly Father, you led your restless and distrustful people in safety through the desert. We pray that you would strengthen and encourage us as we encounter the wilderness, and help us to look to you for our protection and provision. In Jesus' name we pray. Amen

Reading

From the wilderness of Sin the whole congregation of the Israelites journeyed by stages, as the Lord commanded. They camped at Rephidim, but there was no water for the people to drink. The people quarrelled with Moses, and said, '… Why did you bring us out of Egypt, to kill us and our children and livestock with thirst?' So Moses cried out to the Lord, 'What shall I do with this people? They are almost ready to stone me.' The Lord said to Moses, '… Take in your hand the staff with which you struck the Nile, and go. I will be standing there in front of you on the rock at Horeb. Strike the rock, and water will come out of it, so that the people may drink.' Moses did so, in the sight of the elders of Israel.

EXODUS 17:1–6 (ABRIDGED)

Reflection

In this short passage, the tenuous and precarious nature of life in the desert is made clear. Released from slavery in Egypt and pursuing God's promise of the land, the Israelites find themselves without the basic necessity of life—water. 'Distance lends enchantment' goes the saying, and under their present difficulties the people look back with rose-tinted spectacles to their time of captivity, blaming Moses for their predicament. The atmosphere is mutinous and the people's anger with Moses so great that he feels his life could be in danger (v. 4).

There are lessons of trust to be learnt here. In an age when the Spirit of God was believed to work only through the leadership of certain divinely appointed people, it was vital that the Israelites regained their trust in Moses' authority. 'Is the Lord among us or not?' they had asked (v. 7). So Moses is instructed to take some of the elders with him, so that they might see the miracle the Lord was going to perform through him and tell the people what they had witnessed.

Moses, too, was being led into deeper trust. His anxiety in this situation is palpable, and so the Lord gives him clear directions and a strong reaffirmation of his presence: 'I will be there in front of you' (v. 6).

Short silence

Bidding prayers

We offer our prayer to God our loving Father, who lovingly calms our fears and provides for our needs.

Open our hearts, Lord, so that our fears and anxieties may be transformed into a deeper trust in you.
From the stoniness of our hearts, bring forth your living water.

Open our hearts, Lord, so that we may see and gladly respond to the needs of others.
From the stoniness of our hearts, bring forth your living water.

Open our hearts, Lord, so that we may see your love at work in the world around us.
From the stoniness of our hearts, bring forth your living water.

Open our hearts, Lord, so that we may have the courage to lead and the willingness to be led.
From the stoniness of our hearts, bring forth your living water.

Collect

Gracious Father,
you patiently coax your children
into grateful response
through all their petulant rebellion.
When we fear the unknown future,
forgive our mistrust of your loving guidance;
help us to drink deeply of the living water
flowing out of the rock which is
Jesus Christ our Lord.
Amen

The Fourth Sunday of Lent

Opening prayer

Almighty God, you are light, and in you there is no darkness at all. Give us, we pray, a passionate humility that takes Jesus as its pattern, that we may offer our whole being to the service of Christ and his kingdom. We ask this in Jesus' name. Amen

Reading

Be imitators of God, as beloved children, and live in love, as Christ loved us and gave himself up for us, a fragrant offering and sacrifice to God… For once you were darkness, but now in the Lord you are light. Live as children of light—for the fruit of the light is found in all that is good and right and true. Try to find out what is pleasing to the Lord. Take no part in the unfruitful works of darkness, but instead expose them. For it is shameful even to mention what such people do secretly; but everything exposed by the light becomes visible, for everything that becomes visible is light. Therefore it says, 'Sleeper, awake! Rise from the dead, and Christ will shine on you.'

EPHESIANS 5:1–2, 8–14

Reflection

There are many sympathetic vibrations here with other New Testament material: the striking juxtaposition of light and darkness resonating with John's Gospel; Jesus' followers as the light of the world (Matthew 5:14); the references to fruit and fruitfulness (John 15; Galatians 5).

All of these glittering facets undergird the urgent injunction, 'Be imitators of God.' How do we do this? Clearly, states the writer, by modelling our lives on Jesus, who 'loved us and gave himself up for us' (v. 2).

What follows could be misunderstood as simply a prescriptive approach to behaviour: do this, don't do that, find out what God wants and behave accordingly. But this approach had already been tried many times in Israel's history and had been found wanting.

We need to look deeper. The imitation we are urged to attempt is of the one who gave up his life for us, 'a fragrant offering and sacrifice to God' (v. 2). Truly to imitate Jesus is to walk in the way of sacrifice and of 'passionate humility',[4] a quality that is light years away from either a cringing inferiority or the arrogant pseudo-humility of a Uriah Heep. True humility involves a realistic acceptance of ourselves and our place in the scheme of things—our human frailty and our God-given giftedness placed at his disposal in the service of his kingdom.

Short silence

Bidding prayers

We bring our prayers to God, our Creator and Redeemer, who knows the truth of our hearts and loves us with an everlasting love.

In your strength, O Lord, may we find the courage to resist the world's compromises.
Help us, O Lord, to live as children of the light.

In your strength, O Lord, may we renounce our greed and take no more than we need of the world's resources.
Help us, O Lord, to live as children of the light.

In your strength, O Lord, may we hold back from unthinking and hurtful talk that damages the lives of others.
Help us, O Lord, to live as children of the light.

In your strength, O Lord, may we live our lives with open, generous and thankful hearts.
Help us, O Lord, to live as children of the light.

Collect

Almighty God,
you call us out of darkness
to live as children of light.
Give us the humility to face and accept the truth
of our flawed humanity,
that we may gladly take up our cross
and follow the Christ-path
with thankfulness and joy.
In Jesus' name we pray,
Amen

The Fifth Sunday of Lent (Passiontide begins)

Opening prayer

Dear Lord and heavenly Father, lead us, we pray, in the way of the cross. Encourage our faint hearts with the promise of your presence, that we may walk with Christ the road that leads to our salvation. We ask this in Jesus' name. Amen

Reading

They were on the road, going up to Jerusalem, and Jesus... took the twelve aside again and began to tell them what was to happen to him, saying, 'See, we are going up to Jerusalem, and the Son of Man will be handed over to the chief priests and the scribes, and they will condemn him to death; then they will hand him over to the Gentiles; they will... kill him; and after three days he will rise again.' James and John, the sons of Zebedee... said to him, '... Grant us to sit, one at your right hand and one at your left, in your glory.' But Jesus said to them, 'You do not know what you are asking...' When the ten heard this, they began to be angry with James and John. So Jesus called them and said to them, '... Whoever wishes to be first among you must be slave of all. For the Son of Man came not to be served but to serve, and to give his life a ransom for many.'

MARK 10:32–38, 41–45 (ABRIDGED)

Reflection

For the third time, Jesus attempts to prepare his disciples for his coming passion and death. The task is urgent: they are now actually on their way up to Jerusalem for the Passover festival.

The disciples seem not to respond to Jesus directly; perhaps their fear and amazement (v. 32) still prevent them from engaging with the frightening truth. What is offered, obliquely and jarringly, is a request from James and John, who are openly vying for the places of honour in Christ's kingdom. The reaction of the other disciples is one of angry criticism: who do they think they are? We may well share that reaction: after all, their request makes their failure to grasp the truth about Jesus abundantly clear, doesn't it?

But our reaction also makes clear *our* failure to understand, and Jesus' teaching brings the flawed motives of us all into sharp and uncomfortable relief. There is no place in the kingdom for any jostling for position or any privilege snatched at the expense of another. With the original disciples we find ourselves learning, again and again, that following Jesus involves a total renunciation of all our deeply ingrained ideas about power and powerlessness, honour and dishonour. Our habitual sense of personal entitlement is challenged at its very roots.

Short silence

Bidding prayers

We offer our prayers to God, who alone can give us the grace and strength to walk in the way of the cross.

Forgive us, Father, for the times we assume a sense of entitlement over and against others.

Teach us, O Lord, of the power that is made perfect in weakness.

Forgive us, Father, for the times we have bolstered our own security at the expense of others.

Teach us, O Lord, of the power that is made perfect in weakness.

Forgive us, Father, for the times we look for reassurance to the approval of others.

Teach us, O Lord, of the power that is made perfect in weakness.

Forgive us, Father, for the times we opt for the broad highway rather than the narrow way.

Teach us, O Lord, of the power that is made perfect in weakness.

Collect

Living Lord,
who, through your loving, longing and letting go,
discerned that you and your Father were one;
by your courage and example
enable us to respond fearlessly to the Father's love.
May we know him to be the fulfilment of our deepest desires,
where all that is most precious to us
finds its true place and perfection.
We make our prayer through you, our Lord and Saviour.
Amen

Palm Sunday and Holy Week

We enter with Christ the final, harrowing week of his earthly life. As we do so, we are invited to ponder these events through the experiences of some of those most intimately involved, and to meditate on the worst—and the best—of which our frail human nature is capable.

Palm Sunday

Opening prayer

Almighty God, we stand with Christ at the beginning of the last week of his earthly life. As we lay our palms at his feet, we pray that we may faithfully follow in his footsteps to the cross and all that lies beyond. Amen

Reading

The next day the great crowd that had come to the festival heard that Jesus was coming to Jerusalem. So they took branches of palm trees and went out to meet him, shouting, 'Hosanna! Blessed is the one who comes in the name of the Lord—the King of Israel!' Jesus found a young donkey and sat on it; as it is written: 'Do not be afraid, daughter of Zion. Look, your king is coming, sitting on a donkey's colt!' His disciples did not understand these things at first; but when Jesus was glorified, then they remembered... So the crowd that had been with him when he called Lazarus out of the tomb and raised him from the dead continued to testify... The Pharisees then said to one another, 'You see, you can do nothing. Look, the world has gone after him!'
JOHN 12:12–19 (ABRIDGED)

Reflection

For its celebration of Jesus' entry into Jerusalem, the Church has taken over the practice of the waving of palm branches, a tradition found only in John's Gospel. The Gospel writer's recording of this event is heavy with anticipation and foreboding: the crowd cheering Jesus' entry had witnessed the raising of Lazarus and is expecting more wonders (v. 17), and the authorities are getting increasingly nervous as events spiral out of their control (v. 19).

John describes the crowd being swept along on a great tide of excitement and high expectation—a state which Jesus' choice of a young donkey (rather than a war-horse) as his mount does nothing to dispel. Huge claims are being made: Jesus is 'the one who comes in the name of the Lord—the King of Israel!' No wonder the authorities are nervous.

But none of them—the religious authorities, the disciples or the crowd—are yet in a position to understand the full significance of Jesus' actions. It will only be in the light of the crucifixion and resurrection that his unique pattern of self-giving messiahship will begin to make sense (v. 16).

It is from this mysterious blend of majesty and loving humility that the Church derives its life. Two thousand years on, we continue to remember, and ponder the mystery.

Short silence

Bidding prayers

We bring our prayers and concerns to our loving Father, offering ourselves for the service of his kingdom.

For the nations of the world; that we may cease our grasping after power and earthly security.
Strengthen us, O Lord, that we may walk in the way of the cross.

For the holy Church of God; that we may resist the lure of earthly recognition and approval.
Strengthen us, O Lord, that we may walk in the way of the cross.

For our families and local communities; that we may relate to one another in love and mutual support.
Strengthen us, O Lord, that we may walk in the way of the cross.

For ourselves and our walk with Christ; that we may be led ever more deeply into the heart of his sacrificial love.
Strengthen us, O Lord, that we may walk in the way of the cross.

Collect

Lord Jesus Christ,
as you entered Jerusalem
the crowds acclaimed you King.
May we lay our palms before you
and kneel in worship at your feet,
seeing in your humble majesty
the source of our life and our salvation.
We ask this in your precious name.
Amen

Monday of Holy Week
(Mary of Bethany)

Opening prayer

Holy God, we open our hearts to you in praise and gratitude. May the humble offering of our lives be as precious ointment poured out in the service of your love. We ask this in Jesus' name. Amen

Reading

Six days before the Passover Jesus came to Bethany, the home of Lazarus, whom he had raised from the dead. There they gave a dinner for him. Martha served, and Lazarus was one of those at the table with him. Mary took a pound of costly perfume made of pure nard, anointed Jesus' feet, and wiped them with her hair... But Judas Iscariot... said, 'Why was this perfume not sold for three hundred denarii and the money given to the poor?' ... Jesus said, 'Leave her alone. She bought it so that she might keep it for the day of my burial. You always have the poor with you, but you do not always have me.'

JOHN 12:1–8 (ABRIDGED)

Reflection

The Synoptic Gospels preserve two anointing traditions. Mark 14:3–9 records the actions of an anonymous woman, associating her anointing of Jesus with his imminent suffering and as a preparation for his burial. A second tradition, found in Luke 7:36–49, has no connection with Jesus' suffering and death, and is linked instead to a trenchant lesson in forgiveness.

Elements of both are found in this incident in John, and, as in Mark, it is directly linked with Jesus' death. But there are hidden signs here, of whose significance we may not be aware but which add layers of enrichment and depth to the story's meaning. Mary anoints Jesus' feet and wipes them with her hair. While some scholars have suggested that this detail is alien to the style of John's Gospel and has no real significance in the story, others have argued that it is crucial. Gail O'Day points out that the verb 'to wipe' (*ekmasso*) is the same as that used to describe Jesus' wiping of the disciples' feet after the foot-washing. This extravagant anointing is therefore rich with symbolic foreshadowing—of Jesus' passion and death, certainly, but also of the ongoing life of loving mutual service that is to be the benchmark of the Christian community. What the disciples had to be taught by clear object lesson, Mary seems to know instinctively. 'She embraces Jesus' departure… before he has taught his followers about its true meaning.'[5]

Short silence

Bidding prayers

We come before God with our prayers and thanksgiving, seeking his gifts of love and humility in the life of the world.

We live in a world of great need. Show us, O Lord, how we may more willingly serve.
Deepen in us, O Lord, your way of service and sacrificial love.

We live in a world marked by massive inequality of resources. Show us, O Lord, how we may more freely give.
Deepen in us, O Lord, your way of service and sacrificial love.

We live in a world obsessed with the need to possess. Show us, O Lord, how we may share with delight in the gifts of your creation.
Deepen in us, O Lord, your way of service and sacrificial love.

We live in a world that puts us under constant pressure to conform. Show us, O Lord, how we may grow to maturity in your love.
Deepen in us, O Lord, your way of service and sacrificial love.

Collect

Heavenly Father,
we are undeserving of your blessing,
yet you pour upon us
your abundant gifts of love.
Accept, we pray,
the trembling efforts of our hearts,
and transform them into sweet fragrance
offered for your glory.
We ask this for Jesus' sake.
Amen

Tuesday of Holy Week
(Simon Peter)

Opening prayer

*Almighty God, as we stand with Peter in his time of crisis, we
know only too well the weakness of our own resolve. May we have
the integrity to face our failures and the courage to trust in your
forgiveness and restoration. We ask this in Jesus' name. Amen*

Reading

'Simon, Simon, listen! Satan has demanded to sift all of you
like wheat, but I have prayed for you that your own faith
may not fail; and you, when once you have turned back,
strengthen your brothers.' And he said to him, 'Lord, I am
ready to go with you to prison and to death!' Jesus said,
'I tell you, Peter, the cock will not crow this day, until you
have denied three times that you know me.'

LUKE 22:31–34

Reflection

As Holy Week progresses, so the intensity of the conflict
surrounding Jesus and his disciples continues. This passage
follows immediately after Luke's presentation of the discussion about greatness among the disciples, and Peter still feels
confident. Jesus is more realistic, and his reference to Satan's
demand to sift the disciples like wheat is reminiscent of
Satan's testing of Job (Job 1:11–12). This testing is going to
challenge Peter to the utmost: will he be up to the task?

Jesus is shockingly blunt about the catastrophic depths to which Peter's failure will take him (v. 34), and yet this despair contains within it a seed of hope: 'and you, when once you have turned back, strengthen your brothers' (v. 32). Here, surely, is hope for us all. We know what it is like to overestimate our capabilities. We know, also, the feelings of guilt and shameful inadequacy that can overwhelm us when we let others down and fail to live up to our own high expectations.

Jesus knows that the disciple will not always be faithful, and this is as true today as it was for Peter. But is this the final word? Equally true for us are the opportunity and task that lie beyond our failure (v. 32). We will fail, repeatedly; but, like Peter, we have the opportunity to 'turn back' and continue the journey.

Short silence

Bidding prayers

We bring our prayers to our loving Father, seeking his strength in times of crisis and his forgiveness and renewal when we fail.

We seek your mercy, Lord, for those times when our courage has failed us and we have not stood as faithful witnesses to you.
Forgive us, Lord, we pray, and restore us in your love.

We seek your courage, Lord, to own our failures and to seek your forgiveness with humility and gratitude.
Forgive us, Lord, we pray, and restore us in your love.

We seek your mercy, Lord, for those times when our courage has failed and we have not supported those who depend on us.

Forgive us, Lord, we pray, and restore us in your love.

We seek your courage, Lord, to own our failures and to seek forgiveness and restoration in our damaged relationships.

Forgive us, Lord, we pray, and restore us in your love.

Collect

Lord Jesus Christ,
you saw in Simon Peter
both the cowardice of one deeply afraid
and the strength and inspiration
that would build your Church.
May we take courage from his example,
and enable us to know that if we 'turn back',
you still have work for us to do
in the silent growth of your kingdom.
We ask this in your name.
Amen

Wednesday of Holy Week
(Pontius Pilate)

Opening prayer

Heavenly Father, we pray that you will help us to grow into wholeness in your presence, neither denying our weaknesses nor overplaying our strengths. We praise your name, O Lord, for all that we have and are is your gift. In Jesus' name we pray. Amen

Reading

Pilate then called together the chief priests, the leaders, and the people, and said to them, 'You brought me this man as one who was perverting the people; and here I have examined him in your presence and have not found this man guilty of any of your charges against him. Neither has Herod, for he sent him back to us. Indeed, he has done nothing to deserve death. I will therefore have him flogged and release him…' But they kept urgently demanding with loud shouts that he should be crucified; and their voices prevailed.

LUKE 23:13–16, 23

Reflection

Nobody (other than Jesus himself) comes out of this incident with any credit. The chief priests and leaders of the people are pictured working the crowd up to a fever-pitch of bloodlust; the crowd then respond as a baying mob, bereft of any vestige of sensibility or compassion. Pilate cannot find Jesus guilty but, in the end, allows himself to be manipulated by more insistent voices and hands him over to be crucified. Other Gospel accounts add all-too-human details: in Matthew, Pilate ignores his wife's warning that he should have nothing to do with Jesus (27:19) and washes his hands of the matter when he fails to convince the crowd (v. 24). John's Gospel adds a note of political and maybe personal threat: 'If you release this man, you are no friend of the emperor' (19:12).

While we may deplore the weakness of Pilate, the particular emphasis given in these accounts has had appalling consequences. The scapegoating of the Jewish people down the centuries, inside and outside the Christian Church, has led to cruelty and atrocities beyond our imagining.

The point of these accounts is not to demonise any particular individual or racial group. Rather, we are invited to stand alongside each person represented here—Pilate, chief priest and crowd member—and ponder the awful certainty that, given the 'right' conditions, we too would have been, and are, capable of such behaviour.

Short silence

Bidding prayers

Knowing our humanity, our frequent cowardice and certainty of being right, we bring our prayers before our heavenly Father.

When we are tempted to ignore issues of injustice:
Lord, with your leading, may we resist the pressure of the crowd and stand up for what is right.

When we are tempted to take the way of least resistance:
Lord, with your leading, may we resist the pressure of the crowd and stand up for what is right.

When we are tempted to remain silent rather than speak your truth:
Lord, with your leading, may we resist the pressure of the crowd and stand up for what is right.

When we are tempted to speak in pious self-justification rather than take the costly way of love:
Lord, with your leading, may we resist the pressure of the crowd and stand up for what is right.

Collect

Heavenly Father,
there are times
when we find it all too easy to go with the crowd,
and to wash our hands
of matters that cause us discomfort.
Chasten our self-righteousness, we pray,
and in your strength
may we find the courage
to face the weaknesses of our common humanity.
We ask this for Jesus' sake.
Amen

Maundy Thursday
(Judas Iscariot)

Opening prayer

Heavenly Father, on this night you shared a final supper with your disciples and, through the washing of their feet, set out the pattern of your kingship. Give us the courage, Lord, to see these events through the eyes of Judas and to recognise within ourselves our own potential for betrayal. We ask this in Jesus' name. Amen

Reading

After saying this Jesus was troubled in spirit, and declared, 'Very truly, I tell you; one of you will betray me.' The disciples looked at one another, uncertain of whom he was speaking... Jesus [said], 'It is the one to whom I give this piece of bread when I have dipped it in the dish.' So when he had dipped the piece of bread, he gave it to Judas son of Simon Iscariot. After he received the piece of bread, Satan entered into him... [Judas] immediately went out. And it was night.

JOHN 13:21–22, 26–27, 30

Reflection

'After saying this...' These words are vital to our grasp of the full horror of what follows. They lead us on directly from the foot-washing and last supper and make clear that Judas' betrayal arose from within the very heart of this intimate fellowship.

What *was* going on in Judas' mind? Frustration and disappointment, perhaps, that Jesus was clearly not going to be the kind of Messiah he had hoped for? Maybe it was a desperate attempt to manipulate events in order to force Jesus' hand—to make him stand up and actively resist those who were determined to kill him. Or perhaps Judas was never fully committed to Jesus in the way that the other disciples were. The accounts are ambivalent, but clearly he was not always regarded as treacherous (Luke 6:16), and his responsibility for the common purse (John 13:29) implies a high degree of personal trust.

When things are not working out as we feel they should, we may be tempted to try to manipulate events our way. After all, we know best—don't we? We may not be fully able to understand Judas' reasoning but such a temptation may be uncomfortably familiar to us. Rather than condemn, we would perhaps do better to ponder our own capacity for deviousness. 'There but for the grace of God go I.'

Short silence

Bidding prayers

We bring our prayers to almighty God, who alone can turn our betrayals into joyful and willing submission.

When obsessive concern for our own comfort blinds us to the neediness of others:
Turn us from our darkness, Lord, and lead us in the light of Christ.

When certainty about the rightness of our own perception makes us deaf to any other voice:
Turn us from our darkness, Lord, and lead us in the light of Christ.

When, through weakness or selfishness, we betray those who depend upon us:
Turn us from our darkness, Lord, and lead us in the light of Christ.

When, knowing the wretchedness of our state, we can do nothing but cry for your mercy:
Turn us from our darkness, Lord, and lead us in the light of Christ.

Collect

Loving Saviour,
you know the shadows within us—
the bitterness and petty resentments,
and how hard we find it to forgive.
Master, what have we done?
Forgive our weakness and duplicity,
our cowardice, treachery,
and our failures in loving.
Give us the courage to own our inner darkness
and to bring it to you, the light of the world,
who look on us with acceptance, forgiveness and love.
Amen

Good Friday (Jesus)

Opening prayer

Heavenly Father, strengthen us, we pray, to stand firm and face the events of this day with Christ. Support us when our courage fails, and help us to find our rest in a resolute embracing of his cross. We ask this for Jesus' sake. Amen

Reading

When it was noon, darkness came over the whole land until three in the afternoon. At three o'clock Jesus cried out with a loud voice, 'Eloi, Eloi, lema sabachthani?' which means, 'My God, my God, why have you forsaken me?' When some of the bystanders heard it, they said, 'Listen, he is calling for Elijah.' And someone ran, filled a sponge with sour wine, put it on a stick, and gave it to him to drink, saying, 'Wait, let us see whether Elijah will come to take him down.' Then Jesus gave a loud cry and breathed his last.

MARK 15:33–37

Reflection

'My God, my God, why have you forsaken me?' A quotation from Psalm 22:1, Jesus' shattering cry of dereliction from the cross echoes across time, exploding our spiritual and emotional defences and defying our attempts to keep the searing experience of the passion at a manageable distance. One commentary refers to Jesus 'appearing' to be abandoned by God. We find it difficult to take these words at face value and accept that there might be more to them than mere appearance.

In his book *Entering into the Mind of God*, the priest-theologian Anthony Phillips takes an unflinchingly robust approach, arguing that 'Jesus must face his death alone utterly uncertain as to whether after all his life had any meaning or purpose… instead he faces the reality of that yawning abyss that opens to engulf both his integrity and his belief.'[6] And yet, despite the excruciating depths of Jesus' experience, God is still, for him, 'my' God: there is no denial or renunciation.

It is precisely through this cry of dereliction that the true nature of faith is revealed. True faith is willing to risk everything, even when faced with the death of all that seems to give life meaning. It is only when we make the cry of Jesus our own, willingly embracing his divine impotence on the cross, that the breakthrough to resurrection becomes possible.

Short silence

Bidding prayers

Throughout his agony, Jesus held on to his trust in his heavenly Father. We bring our prayers to God, asking that he would deepen our trust in times of darkness.

When cherished dreams are broken and the future is unclear:
Lord, we cling to you; you have the words of eternal life.

When ambition outstrips ability and the future is unclear:
Lord, we cling to you; you have the words of eternal life.

When others disappoint us and the future is unclear:
Lord, we cling to you; you have the words of eternal life.

When illness confronts us with our mortality and the future is unclear:
Lord, we cling to you; you have the words of eternal life.

Collect

Heavenly Father,
we shrink from Jesus' experience of abandonment,
finding it almost too painful to bear.
Help us, we pray,
to face our own personal abyss with his courage,
resolutely holding to you in the darkness
and trusting you
for a future we cannot see.
In Jesus' name we pray.
Amen

Easter Eve

Opening prayer

Compassionate Father, may our hearts and spirits be open as we reach out to you from a place of darkness and desolation. Amen

Reading

'For there is hope for a tree, if it is cut down, that it will sprout again, and that its shoots will not cease. Though its root grows old in the earth, and its stump dies in the ground, yet at the scent of water it will bud and put forth branches like a young plant. But mortals die, and are laid low; humans expire, and where are they? As waters fail from a lake, and a river wastes away and dries up, so mortals lie down and do not rise again; until the heavens are no more, they will not awake or be roused out of their sleep.'

JOB 14:7–12

Reflection

Despite 2000 years of hindsight, we need today to attempt the impossible. We need to allow ourselves to face what seemed to be the final, tragic reality—that all the promises, all the hopes and dreams invested in Jesus had come to an ignominious end in the vicious barbarity of a Roman crucifixion. The Gospel accounts are spare, bleak: Jesus is laid in the tomb of Joseph of Arimathea, and the women wait until the sabbath is over, when they will be able to anoint his body. There are only two references to any prediction of resurrection, the first looking back to Jesus' own words early in John's Gospel (2:19) and the second from the memory of the religious leaders, who urge Pilate to secure the tomb to prevent Jesus' disciples from taking his body and claiming he has risen (Matthew 27:62–66).

For Jesus' followers, on this day, it must have seemed like the end. This passage from Job must have resonated deeply: a tree, when cut down, may sprout again, but what happens to human beings? Does the regeneration of the felled tree offer us any hope? No, there is no hope: human beings cannot put out new shoots as trees do. There will be no waking for them 'until the heavens are no more' (v. 12).

We need to allow ourselves, today, to really *feel* that sense of hopelessness and desolation.

Short silence

Bidding prayers

We bring our prayers in faith and hope to God, who stands beside us in our darkness.

Father, we feel the depths of pain in your world, and our hearts yearn for healing and resurrection.
We cry to you from out of the depths: O Lord, hear our prayer.

Father, we feel the depths of pain in your Church, and our hearts yearn for healing and resurrection.
We cry to you from out of the depths: O Lord, hear our prayer.

Father, we feel the depths of pain in the lives of those around us, and our hearts yearn for healing and resurrection.
We cry to you from out of the depths: O Lord, hear our prayer.

Father, we feel the depths of pain within ourselves, and our hearts yearn for healing and resurrection.

We cry to you from out of the depths: O Lord, hear our prayer.

Collect

Saviour of the world,
on the cross of death
you plumbed the depths of loss and abandonment.
When we are tempted to despair and hope seems vanquished,
give us grace to believe
that, mysteriously, the very darkness itself
contains the seeds of resurrection and new life.
We make our prayer through you, Lord Jesus,
the light that no darkness can quench.
Amen

Easter

Like the dramatic finale of Beethoven's Ninth Symphony,
the triumphant resurrection of Christ erupts on Easter
morning as a cosmic 'Ode to Joy'. Christ is risen—Alleluia!
But there has been no precedent for this, and those
people tending wounds of shock, guilt and deep sorrow
are initially disoriented. Who is this stranger? Is it the
Lord? The overwhelming, awesome reality of Christ's risen
presence among them will take time to absorb.

Easter Day

Opening prayer

Heavenly Father, we rejoice today and celebrate with all those who worship the risen Christ. As we wonder afresh at the miracle of his resurrection, revive our spirits, we pray, that we may continue to serve you with glad and loving hearts. Amen

Reading

When the sabbath was over, Mary Magdalene, and Mary the mother of James, and Salome bought spices, so that they might go and anoint him… As they entered the tomb, they saw a young man, dressed in a white robe… and they were alarmed. But he said to them, 'Do not be alarmed; you are looking for Jesus of Nazareth, who was crucified. He has been raised; he is not here… But go, tell his disciples and Peter that he is going ahead of you to Galilee; there you will see him, just as he told you. So they went out and fled from the tomb, for terror and amazement had seized them; and they said nothing to anyone, for they were afraid.

MARK 16:1, 5–8 (ABRIDGED)

Reflection

'Alleluia. Christ is risen.'[7] The absence of exclamation marks should not dampen our sense of joy and celebration. Christ *is* risen indeed—alleluia! Most of the Gospel accounts relate the dawning of a stunned, joyful realisation among the disciples as the risen Jesus begins to appear to them (John 20—21; Luke 24:13–53; Matthew 28).

Events have turned out more wonderfully than anyone

had dared hope, and at this point we may be tempted to breathe a collective sigh of relief. The heightened spiritual emotion of Lent and Holy Week is over for another year, and we can relax again as events continue their 'predictable' course. We should not move on too hastily, however, and Mark's account warns us against complacency. Here we find a very different slant to the post-crucifixion events, one which may encourage us to stay with the mystery of the resurrection a little longer.

Christ is risen, but this shorter ending of Mark's Gospel leaves us with a strong sense of fear and uncertainty rather than joy. Christ is risen, but the bewildered women cannot, at this point, take in what that means, and they run away in fear. Christ is risen, and although, with the hindsight of 2000 years, we may have moved beyond the women's 'terror and amazement', we need to remember that the awe and the mystery remain.

Short silence

Bidding prayers

We offer our prayers to our heavenly Father, who brings light out of darkness and life out of death.

Christ is risen: we pray that his disciples may be empowered to live the reality of his risen life in our world.
Infuse our spirits, O God, with the life and power of the risen Christ.

Christ is risen: we pray that his disciples may be empowered to live the reality of his risen life in the Church.
Infuse our spirits, O God, with the life and power of the risen Christ.

Christ is risen: we pray that his disciples may be empowered to live the reality of his risen life in their families and local communities.
Infuse our spirits, O God, with the life and power of the risen Christ.

Christ is risen: we pray that his disciples may be empowered to live the reality of his risen life in their own relationships and personal circumstances.
Infuse our spirits, O God, with the life and power of the risen Christ.

Collect

Heavenly Father,
through the mighty resurrection of your Son
the tide of darkness was turned
and death itself vanquished.
Give us eyes of faith,
that we may see the Christ-light
alive in the darkness of our world,
and that we may gladly share with him
in your mission of love and redemption.
In Jesus' name we pray.
Amen

The Second Sunday of Easter

Opening prayer

Risen Lord Jesus, we pray for a deepening awareness of your presence in all things. May we be open to the miracle of your transforming power in all the ordinary and extraordinary experiences of our lives. Amen

Reading

After these things Jesus showed himself again to the disciples by the Sea of Tiberias; and he showed himself in this way... Simon Peter said to them, 'I am going fishing.' They said to him, 'We will go with you.' They went out and got into the boat, but that night they caught nothing. Just after daybreak, Jesus stood on the beach; but the disciples did not know that it was Jesus. Jesus said to them, 'Children, you have no fish, have you?' They answered him 'No.' He said to them, 'Cast the net to the right side of the boat, and you will find some.' So they cast it, and now they were not able to haul it in because there were so many fish. That disciple whom Jesus loved said to Peter, 'It is the Lord!' When Simon heard that it was the Lord, he put on some clothes, for he was naked, and jumped into the sea. But the other disciples came in the boat, dragging the net full of fish... Jesus said to them, 'Come and have breakfast.' ... Jesus came and took the bread and gave it to them, and did the same with the fish.

JOHN 21:1–8, 12–13 (ABRIDGED)

Reflection

We do not know how many days have elapsed since Jesus last appeared to his disciples, but any excitement engendered by those earlier appearances seems to have evaporated. The mood is listless, even despondent, and the disciples have lost their sense of direction. Peter's announcement that he is going fishing represents a return to the security he knew before he met Jesus, not a patient waiting for what the future might bring.

It is precisely at this point of regression that Jesus meets his disheartened disciples, urging them to let down their net one more time. After a fruitless night's fishing, the disciples may have thought that this would prove pointless, but they do it anyway. There is a lovely irony here: we can almost hear the gentle laughter in Jesus' voice as he says that, if they do what he suggests, they will 'find some'. What they do find is a catch that strains the net beyond what should have been breaking point.

All seems designed to reassure the disciples and get them back on track. The enormous quantity of fish may have resonated with memories of another abundant feeding, where many baskets were needed to gather up the leftovers. And in the simple sharing of breakfast? Perhaps a reminder of a recent Passover meal, and the assurance of Jesus alive and present in the ordinary daily routine of life.

Short silence

Bidding prayers

We bring our prayers to almighty God, who, through Christ, offers us encouragement and hope.

When life seems flat, and without purpose:
Lord Jesus, be our constant presence.

When we are searching for a sense of direction:
Lord Jesus, be our constant presence.

When the hope we had has evaporated like dew at dawn:
Lord Jesus, be our constant presence.

When our souls need deeper roots in the rich soil of your nurturing love:
Lord Jesus, be our constant presence.

Collect

Risen Lord Jesus,
you appeared to your discouraged disciples,
feeding and inspiring them with fresh hope and fervour.
When courage flags and resolve weakens,
come to us in your gentleness, Lord.
Giver of all good gifts, nurture us in our fragility,
and may we know your constant presence
in every aspect of our lives.
In your name we pray.
Amen

The Third Sunday of Easter

Opening prayer

Lord God our Father, we come before you in praise and thanks-
giving. We seek your courage, Lord, to inhabit the gospel you have
given us to live, and the security to allow the freedom of thought
and speech of those who hold views different from our own. We ask
this in Jesus' name. Amen

Reading

While Peter and John were speaking to the people, the
priests, the captain of the temple, and the Sadducees came
to them, much annoyed because they were teaching the
people and proclaiming that in Jesus there is the resurrection
of the dead. So they arrested them and put them in custody
until the next day, for it was already evening. But many of
those who heard the word believed; and they numbered
about five thousand.

ACTS 4:1–4

Reflection

It is still early days, but the Spirit of the risen Jesus is clearly
alive and active in the fledgling Church. The people have
been filled with 'wonder and amazement' at a miracle of
healing accomplished through Peter (Acts 3:1–10), and
his subsequent addressing of the crowd draws many new
believers into the Christian community (vv. 11–26; 4:4).

Already, though, there are worrying intimations of the
dangers that lie ahead for the believers. As implacable oppon-
ents of any idea of resurrection, the Sadducees join with the

priests and captain of the temple guard to try to crush this alarming new development. Peter and John are arrested and committed to prison to give an account of themselves before the authorities the following day.

As we follow the news each day, this account of the attempts of the powers-that-be to suppress ideas and behaviour that they deem threatening to their position has a disturbingly contemporary feel. But as we were reflecting recently (Holy Week: Wednesday), we should again avoid the temptation to make a scapegoat out of one particular racial group. Here, the heavy-handed tactics of the religious authorities in trying to snuff out opposition remind us uncomfortably of our own tendencies to ignore, sideline or actively suppress whatever we feel threatens our personal security and interests. In behaving like this, Israel's religious leaders are simply acting out that tendency on behalf of us all.

Short silence

Bidding prayers

Our heavenly Father is always more ready to hear than we are to pray. So let us offer our prayers to him in confidence and trust.

We pray for all who suffer political or religious persecution.
Lord, may we stand in the freedom you give us, while honouring the freedom of others.

We pray for all who abuse their authority in their oppression of others.
Lord, may we stand in the freedom you give us, while honouring the freedom of others.

We pray for all who believe, that they may live Christ's truth each day.

Lord, may we stand in the freedom you give us, while honouring the freedom of others.

We pray for all who are drawn to Christ by the life and witness of others.

Lord, may we stand in the freedom you give us, while honouring the freedom of others.

Collect

Heavenly Father,
you call us in Christ
to active and fearless discipleship.
Encourage us, we pray, to stand fast
when our faith is met with unbelief,
and yet still to respect and honour
the freedom of the other,
within the love of Christ.
We ask this in Jesus' name.
Amen

The Fourth Sunday of Easter

Opening prayer

Father of all, we pray that you would lead us out of the prison of our fears and insecurities, into the glorious freedom that is your gift to your children. We ask this in Jesus' name. Amen

Reading

Now the whole group of those who believed were of one heart and soul, and no one claimed private ownership of any possessions, but everything they owned was held in common. With great power the apostles gave their testimony to the resurrection of the Lord Jesus, and great grace was upon them all. There was not a needy person among them, for as many as owned lands or houses sold them and brought the proceeds of what was sold. They laid it at the apostles' feet, and it was distributed to each as any had need.

ACTS 4:32–35

Reflection

A few hours before his tragic death in December 1968, the Trappist monk and writer Thomas Merton addressed a gathering of Buddhist and Christian religious at a conference in Bangkok. As part of his talk, he referred to Karl Marx and his vision of a communist state where resources would be shared according to need, not greed. Given the ways of the world and the fallen state of humanity, Merton suggested that the only place where such a vision had even a remote chance of being successfully lived out was in a monastery.

A society obsessed with MPs' expense claims and the size of bankers' bonuses sits very uneasily alongside this picture of the life of the early Christian community as recorded in Acts. As a result, many have deemed it idealistic and unworkable. And yet there are communities today that quietly buck the trend, managing to live simply, hospitably and sustainably and with a strong emphasis on justice, peace and reconciliation. Many, but by no means all, are Christian. Alongside traditional monastic houses there are a variety of lay groups: Iona, the Othona community, the therapeutic community at Pilsdon in Dorset, the Northumbria community, and many others.

Through a shared will and strong sense of God's leading, such groups have proved that it is possible to live in such a way as to meet each person's need without either harming others or exploiting the created world. Dare we allow these experiences to challenge our own patterns of living?

Short silence

Bidding prayers

Our God gives to us without measure and invites us to live generously with his gifts. We bring our prayers to him in humility and thanksgiving.

As members of the world community,
Help us, Lord, to live with gratitude and openhearted generosity.

As citizens of our country,
Help us, Lord, to live with gratitude and openhearted generosity.

As members of our local communities,
Help us, Lord, to live with gratitude and openhearted generosity.

As family members and friends,
Help us, Lord, to live with gratitude and openhearted generosity.

Collect

Loving Father,
you call your children to share with you
in the building of your kingdom on earth.
When our wealth comes at the expense of others,
challenge our fear and selfishness;
teach us to live with open hearts and hands,
so that all may live and thrive
and share in the gifts of your bounty.
In Jesus' name we pray.
Amen

The Fifth Sunday of Easter

Opening prayer

Heavenly Father, you call us to live in ways that reflect the glory and beauty of your Son. We thank you that you love us eternally, even as we are. May we come before you often in silent worship, resting in the healing light of your forgiveness. Amen

Reading

So if you have been raised with Christ, seek the things that are above, where Christ is, seated at the right hand of God. Set your minds on things that are above, not on things that are on earth, for you have died, and your life is hidden with Christ in God…Put to death, therefore, whatever in you is earthly: fornication, impurity, passion, evil desire, and greed…anger, wrath, malice, slander, and abusive language…Do not lie to one another, seeing that you have stripped off the old self with its practices and have clothed yourself with the new self, which is being renewed in knowledge according to the image of its creator.

COLOSSIANS 3:2–5, 8–10 (ABRIDGED)

Reflection

Last week's reading from Acts gave a brief but intense snapshot of the dynamic, inspiring life of the early Christian community. Today's passage from Colossians focuses rather on the shadow side, detailing those all-too-human traits that should have no place in the Christian fellowship. The list is daunting and covers not only sexual sin but also the many other aspects of behaviour that we tend to let pass without too much thought or notice (at least in ourselves!).

The writer is fully aware of the type of behaviour that can result from human sin, but he is doing far more here than simply haranguing his readers with a forbidding list of 'thou shalt not's. We need to begin, as he does, with Christ rather than the sin, because the behaviour the writer is advocating is a possibility only because of our life in Christ, risen and glorified.

'You have died, and your life is hidden with Christ in God' (v. 3). The words evoke a wonderful image of protective, enfolding love. If we hold on to this awesome reality as the focus of our prayer and contemplation, then the soil in which our new life in Christ takes root will be rich and fertile, and our whole being will be gradually 'renewed in knowledge according to the image of its creator' (v. 10).

Short silence

Bidding prayers

We bring our prayers to our heavenly Father, who holds us, in Christ, within his compassionate embrace.

For our living and being in the world, that we may know the hidden Christ in all the joy and pain we see around us.
Encourage us, Lord, for our lives are hidden with Christ in God.

For our living and being in the Church, that we may know the hidden Christ in the joy of our shared worship and the pain of our differences.
Encourage us, Lord, for our lives are hidden with Christ in God.

For our living and being among those we love, and the hurt that sin can cause between us.
Encourage us, Lord, for our lives are hidden with Christ in God.

For our living and being with God, that all we are and all we do may be more deeply rooted in the soil of his love.
Encourage us, Lord, for our lives are hidden with Christ in God.

Collect

Eternal Father,
in Christ you hold us securely
within the circle of your enfolding love.
Within the safety of your embrace,
give us the courage and will
to die to the temptations of the flesh,
that our vision may be renewed
and our lives transformed
by the beauty of your presence.
In Jesus' name we pray.
Amen

The Sixth Sunday of Easter

Opening prayer

Almighty God, as we seek to walk with you this day, help us to take encouragement from all those who have walked the journey of faith before us. We ask this in Jesus' name. Amen

Reading

Therefore, since we are surrounded by so great a cloud of witnesses, let us also lay aside every weight and the sin that clings so closely, and let us run with perseverance the race that is set before us, looking to Jesus the pioneer and perfecter of our faith, who for the sake of the joy that was set before him endured the cross, disregarding its shame, and has taken his seat at the right hand of the throne of God.

HEBREWS 12:1–2

Reflection

The focus on the person of Jesus Christ in last week's reading is explored further in today's passage from Hebrews, and believers of every age are urged to join the letter's recipients in looking to Jesus, 'the pioneer and perfecter' of our faith, as we continue our journey through life. The words contain both warning and encouragement: warning that the path ahead will not be easy, and will need both perseverance and endurance; and encouragement, because we will not be left to struggle unaided or alone.

It is not easy for us today to think of our faith as need-ing perseverance and endurance. The early decades of the Christian Church were scarred by periods of intense persecution, but most of us (in Britain, at least) will probably never suffer persecution for our beliefs. As a result, our faith and church experience may have become a little too comfortable and domesticated.

Hebrews reminds us compellingly that the way of Jesus is the way of the cross and that he is our pattern and inspiration. We have the constant encouragement of the 'cloud of witnesses'—all those who have gone before us and have endured great trials on their journeys of faith (11:4–39). Christ, his work complete, 'has taken his seat at the right hand of the throne of God' (12:2; see Colossians 3:1), and through him we have constant access to the presence of the Father.

Short silence

Bidding prayers

Through Christ we bring our prayers to God our Father, seeking courage as we walk in the way of the cross.

We pray for the Church in places where it is dangerous to be a Christian; that it may witness to Christ with endurance and courage.
Lord, in your mercy, hear our prayer.

We pray for all victims of torture and those who are persecuted for their faith.
Lord, in your mercy, hear our prayer.

We pray for organisations such as Amnesty International and their work in keeping the reality of persecution before the eyes of the world.
Lord, in your mercy, hear our prayer.

We pray for a quickening of our own faith and a renewed intent to persevere in the face of discouragement or difficulty. **Lord, in your mercy, hear our prayer.**

Collect

Heavenly Father,
help us to keep our eyes on Jesus,
the pioneer and perfecter of our faith.
In the company of all who have gone before,
strengthen and encourage us
as we walk in the way of the cross,
and bless us
with the courage and perseverance
that will see our journey to its end.
We ask this in Jesus' name.
Amen

Ascension Day

Opening prayer

Almighty God, through the Spirit of the ascended Christ you call us to share in the work of your kingdom. May our hearts and spirits be open to receive the enabling and encouragement you offer. Amen

Reading

Then [Jesus] said to them, 'These are my words that I spoke to you while I was still with you—that everything written about me in the law of Moses, the prophets, and the psalms must be fulfilled. Then he opened their minds to understand the scriptures, and he said to them, 'Thus it is written, that the Messiah is to suffer and to rise from the dead on the third day, and that repentance and forgiveness of sins is to be proclaimed in his name to all nations, beginning from Jerusalem…' Then he led them out as far as Bethany, and, lifting up his hands, he blessed them. While he was blessing them, he withdrew from them and was carried up into heaven.

LUKE 24:44–47, 50–51

Reflection

When I was a child, I once saw a painting that I have since been unable to trace. It had a religious theme so I was trying very hard not to laugh at it. It showed a bemused group of disciples staring up at a very solid-looking cloud, from which protruded two feet with toes pointing in opposite directions, as if in a child's drawing. It looked, quite frankly, ridiculous.

Classical art has produced a profusion of work on virtually

every aspect of Christ's life: annunciations, depictions of the Madonna and child, nativities and crucifixions abound. Perhaps the comical effect of the painting I saw helps to explain why all the major artists seemed to have avoided trying to depict the ascension.

How *can* we visualise such an event? Even the Gospel writers struggle. Only Luke attempts it, and even here there is a footnote that states, 'Other ancient authorities lack "and was carried up into heaven".' Rather than getting transfixed by the literal, perhaps we do better to ask what the event means.

Jesus does three major things here. He points to the fulfilment in him of what was written in the law and prophets; he reminds the disciples that they are to be witnesses of all that has happened; and finally he blesses them. Christ's work on earth is complete and he entrusts the disciples with his ongoing mission.

Short silence

Bidding prayers

We bring our prayers to God our Father, in the confidence that he knows our every need.

Ascended Lord, you remind us that the teaching of the law and the prophets finds its fulfilment in you.
We are your witnesses: send us out in the power of your love.

Ascended Lord, you call us to be witnesses to your kingdom of justice and peace.
We are your witnesses: send us out in the power of your love.

Ascended Lord, you bless us and equip us to work in your service.
We are your witnesses: send us out in the power of your love.

Ascended Lord, through you we have access to all the blessings of heaven.
We are your witnesses: send us out in the power of your love.

Collect

Almighty Father,
his work on earth complete,
Christ appeared to his disciples
and reminded them of his message of salvation.
Ground us afresh, we pray, in the miraculous reality
of his life and being,
and bless us, that we may with those first disciples
fulfil our part in Christ's continuing mission
with confidence and joy.
We ask this in his precious name.
Amen

The Seventh Sunday of Easter

Opening prayer

Gracious Lord, you call us to your service as believers who are loved by you and held in your loving care. In our churches, help us to pray and live as communities who are held within your secure embrace, as we look to you for our sustenance and direction. In Jesus' name we pray. Amen

Reading

'I ask not only on behalf of these, but also on behalf of those who will believe in me through their word, that they may all be one. As you, Father, are in me and I am in you, may they also be in us, so that the world may believe that you have sent me. The glory that you have given me I have given them, so that they may be one, as we are one, I in them and you in me, that they may become completely one, so that the world may know that you have sent me and have loved them even as you have loved me.'

JOHN 17:20–23

Reflection

On the eve of his crucifixion, these words of Jesus form part of an extended prayer to his Father of extraordinary intensity and intimacy. After an introduction expressing the mutual glorification of Father and Son, the largest part of this first section (17:7–19) concerns Jesus' prayer for his immediate disciples, who are to be entrusted with his continuing work in the world. With today's passage we are drawn directly into that circle of prayer as it widens to embrace all those who will come after, who will believe through the disciples' work.

This dense and complex prayer offers food for endless contemplation, and we consider two morsels here. First, Jesus is entrusting the future community of believers into the loving hands of his Father. This being so, the Church's own perceptions of its success or failure are ultimately far less important than the fact that it remains always, as Jesus has entrusted it, in the loving care of God.

Second, 'we are a community for whom Jesus prays'.[8] If we really live this reality, then our self-definition as a Christian community will change profoundly. What is Jesus praying to the Father on our behalf today? And in what ways would a silent waiting on God in respect of this question renew and redirect our communal life and energies?

Short silence

Bidding prayers

We bring our prayers to our heavenly Father, who calls us to be one in his love.

Renew us, Lord, in our vision of you as the creator and sustainer of our community life.
Unite us in Christ in the love of the Father, so that the world may believe.

Forgive us, Lord, for the ways in which your Church falls short of your vision of unity within the Father's love.
Unite us in Christ in the love of the Father, so that the world may believe.

Compel us, Lord, by the beauty of your presence, that others may be drawn into a vision of God's glory.
Unite us in Christ in the love of the Father, so that the world may believe.

Help us, Lord, to capture a vision of your love embracing the Church in every age.
Unite us in Christ in the love of the Father, so that the world may believe.

Collect

Heavenly Father,
on the night before he died
your dear Son prayed
that those who believed in him should be one.
Forgive our divisions and redirect our energies, we pray,
that your Church may be affirmed in its calling
and all people be drawn
into the circle of your love.
In Jesus' name we pray.
Amen

Pentecost (Whit Sunday)

Opening prayer

Heavenly Father, through your Son Jesus Christ you empowered his disciples with the gift of the Holy Spirit. May our hearts be open to the Spirit's renewing presence, that we may share with the world the blessings of your abiding peace and love. In Jesus' name we pray. Amen

Reading

When it was evening on that day, the first day of the week, and the doors of the house where the disciples had met were locked for fear of the Jews, Jesus came and stood among them and said, 'Peace be with you.' After he said this, he showed them his hands and his side. Then the disciples rejoiced when they saw the Lord. Jesus said to them again, 'Peace be with you. As the Father has sent me, so I send you.' When he had said this, he breathed on them and said to them, 'Receive the Holy Spirit. If you forgive the sins of any, they are forgiven them; if you retain the sins of any, they are retained.'

JOHN 20:19–23

Reflection

This passage offers an intriguing contrast to the drama and fireworks we read of in Acts 2, and each account embodies a slightly different theological understanding. The Lukan material reflects the most familiar chronology—an Easter/Pentecost division that records the coming of the Spirit *after* the resurrection and ascension of Jesus. But John's Gospel takes a different view, seeing the gift of the Spirit and its significance for mission as being inseparably connected to those events.

In John, the Spirit comes as a gift from the risen Christ himself to the fearful disciples. Many of the promises from Jesus' farewell discourse (John 17) are fulfilled in this reading —promises of lives marked by joy and by the gift of Christ's peace. Also present is Christ's commission: the disciples are sent out 'as the Father has sent me' (v. 21). In this context, the power to forgive or retain sins (v. 23) is no arbitrary gesture, dependent on human judgment or misjudgment. In the power of the Spirit, the Church will witness to the love of God in Christ. In doing this, it will make possible the acceptance or rejection of God's love, and it is in the world's choice that the judgment lies. Joy, peace and empowered witness: these are to be the hallmarks shaping the identity of the infant Church and a pledge of Christ's continuing presence within it.

Short silence

Bidding prayers

In the power of the Spirit, we bring our prayers, through Christ, to our heavenly Father.

We pray that we may be your witnesses in the world, seeing always beyond its superficiality.
Breathe on us, Lord, and deepen in us the life of your kingdom.

We pray that we may be your witnesses in the world, seeing always beneath its pain.

Breathe on us, Lord, and deepen in us the life of your kingdom.

We pray that we may be your witnesses in the world, seeing always beyond its beauty.

Breathe on us, Lord, and deepen in us the life of your kingdom.

We pray that we may be your witnesses in the world, pointing always to the love of Christ present in all things.

Breathe on us, Lord, and deepen in us the life of your kingdom.

Collect

Holy Spirit of God,
you catch us unawares and come to us
as gentle breath, as wind and flame.
May our hearts be tuned to your movement within;
infuse our words and our silence with your healing power,
that they may speak to the world
of your peace, your forgiveness and your love.
In Jesus' name we pray.
Amen

Trinity Sunday

Opening prayer

Almighty God, Creator, Redeemer and Sustainer of all life, open our hearts, we pray, to the vibrant mystery of your being. Stir our hearts, engage our minds and enliven our bodies, that our lives may reflect the richness and beauty of your abundant life. Amen

Reading

'I still have many things to say to you, but you cannot bear them now. When the Spirit of truth comes, he will guide you into all the truth; for he will not speak on his own, but will speak whatever he hears, and he will declare to you the things that are to come. He will glorify me, because he will take what is mine and declare it to you. All that the Father has is mine. For this reason I said that he will take what is mine and declare it to you.'

JOHN 16:12–15

Reflection

'The Father incomprehensible, the Son incomprehensible, the Holy Ghost incomprehensible.'[9] Unfortunately, this early attempt to convey something of the mystery of God's trinitarian reality did not help my childhood understanding, and the wryly humorous addition of '... and the whole jolly lot incomprehensible!' by one anonymous joker seemed to affirm my bewilderment.

It was many years before I began to realise that what had felt like a dry piece of doctrine was actually bursting with life and creative energy. Rublev's compelling icon of the Trinity wonderfully suggested a dynamic of loving relationship, and the use of a candle flame by Hildegard of Bingen to suggest the Trinity's three-in-oneness was surprisingly effective. But it was with Alexander Carmichael's *Carmina Gadelica*, a 19th-century collection of poems and prayers from the Scottish highlands and islands, that light really began to dawn. These reflected a much older tradition, passed down by word of mouth for generations. 'Spirit, give me of Thine abundance, / Father, give me of Thy wisdom, / Son, give me in my need...'[10] What leaps off the page is a sense of personal warmth, immediacy and vibrant energy: each person of the Trinity has gifts to bestow and enfolds the believer in a loving, protective embrace. Here is no dry and distant doctrine or stern measure of orthodox belief, but a radiant, mysterious reality, concerned with and deeply involved in every aspect of the believer's life.

Short silence

Bidding prayers

We offer our prayers and thanks to God the Holy Trinity, seeking a deeper immersion in the light and life he brings.

Bless us, O Father, with the gift of your wisdom.
Enliven us, O Lord, in the mysterious reality of your being.

Hold us, O Son, in our poverty and need.
Enliven us, O Lord, in the mysterious reality of your being.

Enrich us, O Spirit, from the storehouse of your abundance.
Enliven us, O Lord, in the mysterious reality of your being.

Enfold us, O Trinity, in the warmth and security of your embrace.
Enliven us, O Lord, in the mysterious reality of your being.

Collect

Blessed Holy Trinity,
eternal dance of light and love,
transform the lifelessness of our souls and bodies
with the energy of your creative fire.
May our lives be caught up anew
into the wonder and mystery of your eternal being:
Life-Maker, Life-Saver, Life-Renewer
from ages past, and into all eternity.
Amen

Ordinary Time after Trinity

After the life-changing, mountain-top experience of Christ's resurrection and his return to the Father, the challenge to us to reflect his transfigured life in Ordinary Time—the generally mundane routine of our daily lives—can be daunting. The main action of the drama may be over and its tension eased, but God continues to call and equip, as he did John the Baptist, Samuel, Abraham and others. We may feel that nothing much ever happens for us, but the journey in Ordinary Time reminds us that God, in Christ, never ceases to call and inspire.

Trinity 1

Opening prayer

Heavenly Father, we pray that you would give us the grace to hear your voice in our daily lives, and the wisdom to see that your call is not extinguished by difficult circumstances. Amen

Reading

Now the boy Samuel was ministering to the Lord under Eli. The word of the Lord was rare in those days; visions were not widespread… Then the Lord called, 'Samuel! Samuel!' and he said 'Here I am!' and ran to Eli, and said, 'Here I am, for you called me.' But he said, 'I did not call; lie down again.' … The Lord called again… [and] the Lord called Samuel again, a third time. And he got up and went to Eli, and said, 'Here I am, for you called me.' Then Eli perceived that the Lord was calling the boy. Therefore Eli said to Samuel, 'Go, lie down; and if he calls you, you shall say, "Speak, Lord, for your servant is listening."'

1 SAMUEL 3:1, 4–9 (ABRIDGED)

Reflection

Where the call of God is concerned, you're never too young! Samuel, a recently weaned infant, had been left at the temple of Shiloh as a parental thank-offering to God for the miracle of his birth. But all was not well: 'The word of the Lord was rare in those days' (v. 1). The priest Eli was old and weak, and his sons treated the temple and the Lord's offerings with contempt. In this unpromising situation Samuel ministers faithfully, obediently and single-heartedly, neither criticising nor colluding, but quietly persisting with the tasks he has been given.

Then, late one night, comes a voice in the darkness, calling his name: 'Samuel! Samuel!' Alert in an instant, Samuel runs quickly to Eli: 'Here I am, for you called me.' Again, and again, the voice calling… and Samuel's eventual response, at Eli's bidding: 'Speak, Lord, for your servant is listening.'

Like Samuel, we may find ourselves serving God in circumstances not of our choosing. The authority we work under may be weak or corrupt and the things of God misunderstood or dishonoured. But the experience of the young Samuel encourages us to persevere, trusting that no situation, however difficult or painful, has the power to cut us off from the voice of God, who loves us and calls us by name.

Short silence

Bidding prayers

Let us offer our prayers to our heavenly Father, who speaks to us in all the circumstances of our lives.

Lord of all wisdom, you call us to respond to you in times of joy and sorrow. Attune our hearts, we pray, so we may hear your call.
Speak, Lord, for your servant is listening.

Lord of all wisdom, you call us to respond to you in times of ease and struggle. Enable us, we pray, to stay in the place of your choosing.
Speak, Lord, for your servant is listening.

Lord of all wisdom, you call us to respond to you in times of justice and injustice. Help us discern, we pray, when to speak and when to be silent.

Speak, Lord, for your servant is listening.

Lord of all wisdom, you call us to respond to you in times of security and insecurity. Help us to trust, we pray, that we rest secure in your care.

Speak, Lord, for your servant is listening.

Collect

Heavenly Father,
in the darkness of the night
you called the child Samuel
and equipped him for your service.
In the silence of our hearts
help us to wait on you with loving attentiveness;
give us ears to hear your call
and a willingness to share in the work of your kingdom.
Through Jesus Christ our Lord,
Amen

Trinity 2

Opening prayer

Almighty God, open our hearts to the magnitude of your promises and the richness of the blessings you pour upon us. We ask this in Jesus' name. Amen

Reading

And the Lord said to Abram, 'Go from your country and your kindred and your father's house to the land that I will show you. I will make of you a great nation, and I will bless you, and make your name great, so that you will be a blessing. I will bless those who bless you, and the one who curses you I will curse; and in you all the families of the earth shall be blessed.'

GENESIS 12:1–3

Reflection

Where the call of God is concerned, you're never too old! Having reached the age of 75, Abraham could perhaps be forgiven for thinking that the time for setting out into the unknown was past, but God had other ideas. 'Go from your country and your kindred and your father's house to the land that I will show you,' came the command, accompanied by a promise of unimaginable blessing.

It is human nature to want to stay where we feel secure, but the kind of settled comfort we may be happy with can make us complacent and shut us off from the voice of God. If we are serious in our commitment, we can expect to be exposed to the probing, often disturbing Holy Spirit within, calling us to ever-deeper response. We will be challenged to trust more fully in the God who loves us too deeply to leave us within the supposed security of our limited horizons. We are called to trust God with our deepest selves and all we hold most dear, and many times we will hesitate on the brink. But with God's challenge comes this promise: as we respond to his call, his blessing will be with us, and he will lead us into a future beyond our wildest dreams.

Short silence

Bidding prayers

We bring our prayers to God, who calls and equips us to take our part in his creative work.

God of all time and place, we pray for our world: give to those who are called to lead a vision of your glorious purposes:
Hear us, we pray, Lord; and help us to listen.

God of all time and place, we pray for our country: give to those who lead a vision for the common good:
Hear us, we pray, Lord; and help us to listen.

God of all time and place, we pray for our communities: give to those who lead a vision for friend and neighbour:
Hear us, we pray, Lord; and help us to listen.

God of all time and place, we pray for ourselves: give us a vision of what is possible within the security of your call:
Hear us, we pray, Lord; and help us to listen.

Collect

Almighty God,
you called Abraham from the security of home and family
to follow you into the unknown.
Inspire us with your Spirit of love and trust,
that we may fearlessly respond to your call
and follow you wherever you may lead.
We ask this in Jesus' name.
Amen

Trinity 3

Opening prayer

Heavenly Father, your Son Jesus Christ reached out to the lonely and dispossessed, the troubled and the outcast. We pray that you would give us hospitable hearts so that, in our lives, friend and stranger may find an equal welcome. We ask this for Jesus' sake. Amen

Reading

After this [Jesus] went out and saw a tax collector named Levi, sitting at the tax booth; and he said to him, 'Follow me.' And he got up, left everything, and followed him. Then Levi gave a great banquet for him in his house; and there was a large crowd of tax collectors and others sitting at the table with them. The Pharisees and their scribes were complaining to his disciples, saying, 'Why do you eat and drink with tax collectors and sinners?' Jesus answered, 'Those who are well have no need of a physician, but those who are sick; I have come to call not the righteous but sinners to repentance.'

LUKE 5:27–32

Reflection

The call of Levi follows a similar pattern to the call of the fishermen (Matthew 4:18–22). In both, Jesus' abrupt call to follow leads to an immediate departure from their previous occupations.

Christ's call to discipleship—then and now—contains another, implicit challenge: the call to radical hospitality. Before

Jesus' call, Levi was receiving 'guests' at his tax booth and taking payment from them. We don't know whether he was also lining his own pockets, as so many others did. What is clear, though, is that after his call there is a shift of emphasis. Again we see Levi the host, not at his tax booth but at a banquet thrown in Jesus' honour, to which a large crowd of tax collectors and other undesirables was also invited. Jesus is content in their company, rebuking the religious leaders who challenge him.

We both long for and fear human contact, and Jesus' openness to the sinner and the outcast was a constant threat to the religious leaders' fearful insularity. But the call to openness to others is not optional to discipleship: as Jesus demonstrates, it is at its very heart. Two present-day Benedictines articulate our difficulty well: 'We both want and fear connecting with each other... Our minds cannot conceive of solutions to our dilemma until our hearts are convinced to love.'[11] Only Christ can do the convincing.

Short silence

Bidding prayers

We bring our prayers to God our Father, knowing that we find a welcome in his hospitable heart.

We are often afraid to open the doors of our heart, fearful that we will be overwhelmed.
As we have received, Lord, so may we welcome.

We are often unwilling to reach out, fearful that we will be hurt.
As we have received, Lord, so may we forgive.

We are often constrained in our generosity, fearful that we will not have enough.
As we have received, Lord, so may we give.

We are often afraid to expose our vulnerability, fearful that we will be misunderstood.
As we have received, Lord, so may we love.

Collect

Loving Lord Jesus,
you offered friend and stranger an equal welcome.
May we be so transformed
by the power and gentleness of your love
that we may sensitively and fearlessly reach out to others,
trusting in your love to uphold and sustain.
For your name's sake we pray.
Amen

Trinity 4

Opening prayer

Loving God, we pray that our hearts and lives this day may be attuned to the promptings of the Spirit, and that we may be inspired by the example of your Son, Jesus Christ our Lord. Amen

Reading

One sabbath he was going through the cornfields; and as they made their way his disciples began to pluck heads of grain. The Pharisees said to him, 'Look, why are they doing what is not lawful on the sabbath?' And he said to them, 'Have you never read what David did when he and his companions were hungry and in need of food? He entered the house of God, when Abiathar was high priest, and ate the bread of the Presence, which it is not lawful for any but the priests to eat, and he gave some to his companions.' Then he said to them, 'The sabbath was made for humankind, and not humankind for the sabbath; so the Son of Man is lord even of the sabbath.'

MARK 2:23–28

Reflection

'Love God and do what you like.' I remember feeling a certain amount of scepticism when I first came across this quotation from St Augustine many years ago; surely it was a licence for anarchy—doing your own thing and using God's name as a stamp of approval.

It isn't anything of the kind, of course. People who argue for licence to do what they want may be quick to quote the words about the sabbath being made for people, not people for the sabbath. But the words that follow are usually ignored: 'so the Son of Man is lord even of the sabbath' (v. 28). These words take us to the very heart of the truth Jesus is trying to teach. The freedom he is talking about is a freedom that can only come as a person allows their spiritual roots to be drawn ever deeper into God. It involves an intent and increasingly silent listening, a persistent and careful attention to the delicate movements of the Spirit within our hearts and lives. This is a lifelong process, but the further we journey along this path, the more truthfully and instinctively will we be able to 'love God and do what [we] like', because the will of God and the will of the deeply praying person increasingly converge.

Short silence

Bidding prayers

We bring our prayers before our heavenly Father, knowing that he will hear, and asking that we may listen for his response within our hearts.

When fear and anxiety keep us behind the bars of our inner prisons,
Help us, Lord, to grow in the freedom of the children of God.

When arrogance causes us to assert our will, claiming it to be yours,
Help us, Lord, to grow in the freedom of the children of God.

When uncertainty makes us hesitant and afraid we may 'get it wrong',

Help us, Lord, to grow in the freedom of the children of God.

When prejudice makes us hidebound and too willing to criticise others,

Help us, Lord, to grow in the freedom of the children of God.

Collect

Almighty God,
through the kaleidoscopic mosaic of our lives
you teach us to respond
to the promptings of your Spirit.
May our spirits be shaped
by the teaching and example of your Son,
and may we taste the freedom
that comes from knowing that we are your children,
safe in the security of your love.
We ask this in Jesus' name.
Amen

Trinity 5

Opening prayer

Dear Lord, we thank you that you are a God who is present with us in all the unpredictable circumstances of our lives. Help us, we pray, with the aid of your Spirit, to move with the flow of life's pattern, trusting you for our direction and future. Amen

Reading

Naomi said to her two daughters-in-law, 'Go back each of you to your mother's house. May the Lord deal kindly with you, as you have dealt with the dead and with me. The Lord grant that you may find security, each of you in the house of your husband.' Then she kissed them, and they wept aloud… Orpah kissed her mother-in-law, but Ruth clung to her… Ruth said, 'Do not press me to leave you or to turn back from following you! Where you go, I will go; where you lodge, I will lodge; your people shall be my people, and your God my God.'

RUTH 1:8–9, 14–16 (ABRIDGED)

Reflection

With both her sons dead, Naomi urges her daughters-in-law, Orpah and Ruth, to return to their family homes to find new husbands. Neither woman wishes to leave Naomi but, at her urging and with many tears, Orpah returns to her country and her people. Yet Ruth refuses to go, and decisively binds her future to that of Naomi.

Ruth's decision displays a quiet insistence that speaks of knowing the path she must take. A future with Naomi offered no obvious hope: Ruth was apparently throwing away any chance of finding the security of another husband and home. Yet it was precisely this decision that led to her meeting and marrying Boaz, Naomi's kinsman; and their son Obed became the father of Jesse and grandfather of David.

Sometimes we are called to set aside our personal plans and commit our energies in other directions. Perhaps we need to take on the care of elderly parents, meet the unexpected need of a child in difficulty, or face the sudden loss of a job. This may be unwelcome and give rise to conflicting emotions, with feelings of anger and resentment mixed in with our love and concern. But the message of Ruth encourages us to face the present reality with courage, trusting that there is in Christ, in even the darkest of situations, promise and hope for the future.

Short silence

Bidding prayers

We bring our prayers to God, asking that he would help us to grow in our awareness of his abiding presence in our lives.

Lord of all compassion, we pray for all whose lives have been torn apart by the ravages of war or natural disaster:
Heavenly Father, lead us and hold us in the light of your Spirit.

Lord of all love, we pray for all whose future hopes have been wrecked by bereavement or personal tragedy:
Heavenly Father, lead us and hold us in the light of your Spirit.

Lord of all knowing, we pray for all who find it hard to trust in a future they cannot see or imagine:
Heavenly Father, lead us and hold us in the light of your Spirit.

Lord of all goodness, we pray for those who seek your courage to step out into the unknown:
Heavenly Father, lead us and hold us in the light of your Spirit.

Collect

Heavenly Father,
you called Ruth to live with a people not her own
and, through her faithfulness,
to discover her unique role in your unfolding plan.
Give us, we pray, the trust and freedom
to meet life's challenges,
that we may know, in Christ,
a future and a hope.
In Jesus' name we pray.
Amen

Trinity 6

Opening prayer

Creator God, the universe is alive with your beauty. We pray that you would refresh our vision this day, that we may discern your presence in the places we go and the people and situations we meet. We ask this in Jesus' name. Amen

Reading

By the word of the Lord his works are made; and all his creatures do his will... The Lord has not empowered even his holy ones to recount all his marvellous works, which the Lord the Almighty has established so that the universe may stand firm in his glory. He searches out the abyss and the human heart; he understands their innermost secrets. For the Most High knows all that may be known; he sees from of old the things that are to come. He discloses what has been and what is to be, and he reveals the traces of hidden things. No thought escapes him, and nothing is hidden from him. He has set in order the splendours of his wisdom; he is from all eternity one and the same.

ECCLESIASTICUS 42:15, 17–21

Reflection

Written around 200 years before the birth of Christ, Ecclesiasticus, or The Wisdom of Jesus Son of Sirach, is part of the Old Testament Apocrypha (see Introduction). The passage quoted here recalls both the account in Genesis where God speaks the creation into being (Genesis 1), and the Prologue of John's Gospel, where it is declared that all things were created through God's Word (1:3). Today's passage forms part of an exultant paean of praise to the wonders of creation, and sees the hand of God indelibly imprinted upon everything that is. 'He searches out the abyss and the human heart' (v. 18): this God has created an infinity of space both without and within, infusing the whole with life and energy, and moving through all with boundless freedom.

Scientific discoveries in recent years have massively increased our knowledge of the physical laws that govern our universe. Some people have suggested that the laws of physics will ultimately be able to explain everything, but surely science can only go so far. Each exciting discovery appears to be undergirded with yet another unfathomable layer of mystery. Despite the passage of time and the huge advances in knowledge since Ecclesiasticus was written, we remain encompassed by a vast and still-mysterious universe. Its existence continues to raise as many questions as it answers, and compels believers to fall to their knees in wonder, humility and praise.

Short silence

Bidding prayers

In humility and trust, we bring our prayers to God our Father.

For all living creatures on earth, in their beauty and difference,
We praise you, Lord, for you are the creator of all things.

For the seasons of the year, in their rhythm and harmony,
We praise you, Lord, for you are the creator of all things.

For all that grows upon the earth, in its diversity and fruitfulness,
We praise you, Lord, for you are the creator of all things.

For our call to stewardship of your creation, that we may honour the trust you place in us,
We praise you, Lord, for you are the creator of all things.

Collect

Lord of creation,
your penetrating gaze of love searches out
the farthest reaches of the universe
and the deepest recesses of the human heart.
Enlighten the eyes of our spirit,
that we may know your presence
in the depths of our being
and see your love reflected
in the face of all living creatures.
We ask this for Jesus' sake.
Amen

Trinity 7

Opening prayer

Heavenly Father, we pray that you would help us to live lives that have your kingdom and values at their centre. In Jesus' name we pray. Amen

Reading

'Do not be afraid, little flock, for it is your Father's good pleasure to give you the kingdom. Sell your possessions, and give alms. Make purses for yourselves that do not wear out, an unfailing treasure in heaven, where no thief comes near and no moth destroys. For where your treasure is, there your heart will be also. Be dressed for action and have your lamps lit; be like those who are waiting for their master to return from the wedding banquet, so that they may open the door for him as soon as he comes and knocks.'

LUKE 12:32–36

Reflection

How contrary to the tendency of human nature is the message of today's reading! 'Do not be afraid, little flock,' says Jesus. Afraid of what? These words come at the climax of a passage in which Jesus has been addressing the problem of basic human anxiety: whether we will have enough to eat and drink or clothes to wear. Jesus is saying: relax, because it is your Father's delight to give you everything you need.

The main problem in our world today, though, at least in the affluent West, is not one of need but of greed. In times of recession we feel we are badly off, but to own even one book makes us rich beyond dreams when compared with the truly poor of the world. Jesus urges his disciples to put God's kingdom first and to make purses for themselves that do not wear out (v. 33). But his words also offer a very concrete challenge to a society that functions not only with 'built-in obsolescence' but with an increasing pressure to buy ever more goods that we don't really need.

Such a mindset, if not resisted, will take us over like a powerful drug. We will never truly find what we are looking for, because our deep cravings for security and happiness can never be satisfied by material things. 'For where your treasure is, there your heart will be also' (v. 34).

Short silence

Bidding prayers

In humility and confidence we bring our prayers before our heavenly Father, trusting him to provide for all our needs.

In our lives, Lord, give us a heart to seek first your kingdom.
For where our treasure is, there our heart will be also.

In our lives, Lord, give us a heart to renounce our selfishness and greed.
For where our treasure is, there our heart will be also.

In our lives, Lord, give us a heart that goes out to the need of the poor.
For where our treasure is, there our heart will be also.

In our lives, Lord, give us a heart that finds its rest in you.
For where our treasure is, there our heart will be also.

Collect

Heavenly Father,
forgive us our selfishness
and lack of trust in your provision.
Enable us, we pray, to release our anxious grasp
on all that is not you.
Teach us to live with simplicity and lightness of spirit,
and give us joyful and generous hearts,
that others may be drawn
into the beauty and warmth of your kingdom.
We ask this in Jesus' name.
Amen

Trinity 8

Opening prayer

Holy God, open our eyes, we pray, to the wonder and glory of your presence in the ordinary rhythms and routines of our daily lives. Make us receptive to your presence and quick to respond to your call. In Jesus' name we pray. Amen

Reading

Moses was keeping the flock of his father-in-law Jethro, the priest of Midian; he led his flock beyond the wilderness, and came to Horeb, the mountain of God. There the angel of the Lord appeared to him in a flame of fire out of a bush; he looked, and the bush was blazing, yet it was not consumed. Then Moses said, 'I must turn aside and look at this great sight, and see why the bush is not burned up.' When the Lord saw that he had turned aside to see, God called to him out of the bush, 'Moses, Moses!' And he said, 'Here I am.' Then he said, 'Come no closer! Remove the sandals from your feet, for the place on which you are standing is holy ground... I am the God of your father, the God of Abraham, the God of Isaac, and the God of Jacob.' And Moses hid his face, for he was afraid to look at God.

EXODUS 3:1–6 (ABRIDGED)

Reflection

Moses' first encounter with the living God of Israel erupts unexpectedly within the ordinary daily routine of his life as a shepherd. As a vanguard, an angel appears to him from within the flame of the burning bush. The angel says nothing himself but presages the voice of God, compelling Moses to reverence and worship and summoning him directly to his task.

This encounter contains a deep and perhaps uncomfortable challenge—one that addresses our tendency, even as believers, to behave as if we are the sole authors and guardians of our own lives and destinies. We like to be in control and we use all kinds of means, conscious and unconscious, to try to remain so, but this incident should convince us of the futility of any such attempt. God may have been unknown to Moses before this, but Moses was certainly not unknown to God, and the call and the task that follow these few verses carry all the weight and authority of a divine imperative. 'There is this One who knows and calls by name, even while we imagine we are unknown and unsummoned,' writes Walter Brueggemann.[12] Are we prepared to let down our guard, relinquish our supposed autonomy and open ourselves to the God who wants to reveal his glory in every 'burning bush' of our daily lives?

Short silence

Bidding prayers

We bring our prayers before our holy God, in faith, humility and trust.

Lord, you offer us the gift of your presence in mountain-top experiences of your love.
We bow before you in awe and wonder, for we stand on holy ground.

Lord, you offer us the gift of your presence in the boring, the ordinary and the mundane.
We bow before you in awe and wonder, for we stand on holy ground.

Lord, you offer us the gift of your presence when our fear keeps us at a distance from you.
We bow before you in awe and wonder, for we stand on holy ground.

Lord, you offer us the gift of your presence when you call us to work for your kingdom.
We bow before you in awe and wonder, for we stand on holy ground.

Collect

Holy and awesome God,
each day you surprise us afresh
with the splendour and beauty of your presence.
As we remove our shoes,
help us to see the glory that surrounds us,
and enable us to respond with joy and courage
to the work you are calling us to do.
We ask this in Jesus' name.
Amen

Trinity 9

Opening prayer

Almighty God, we pray that you would quicken our spirits and open our hearts to the One whose living presence embraces all time and eternity. We ask this in Jesus' name. Amen

Reading

The revelation of Jesus Christ, which God gave him to show his servants what must soon take place; he made it known by sending his angel to his servant John, who testified to the word of God and to the testimony of Jesus Christ... John to the seven churches that are in Asia: Grace to you and peace... from Jesus Christ, the faithful witness, the firstborn of the dead, and the ruler of the kings of the earth. To him who loves us and freed us from our sins by his blood, and made us to be a kingdom, priests serving his God and Father, to him be glory... Look! He is coming with the clouds; every eye will see him, even those who pierced him... 'I am the Alpha and the Omega,' says the Lord God, who is and who was and who is to come, the Almighty.

REVELATION 1:1–9 (ABRIDGED)

Reflection

John announces the book of Revelation as the direct revelation of Jesus Christ, and in it we are taken on a breathless journey through a work unlike any other writing in the New Testament. It carries resonances of the visions in Daniel 7—12, the signs accompanying the giving of the law on Sinai (Exodus 19—20) and the opening chapters of the prophecy of Ezekiel. Despite these resonances, though, Revelation remains distinct. Traditionally classified as an apocalypse (from the Greek meaning 'to uncover', or 'reveal'), it addresses the scope of human history and the end of the world in graphic visionary language. These opening verses present themselves with something of a verbal fanfare, and we are swept through the saving work of Jesus on earth to the 'Look! He is coming with the clouds...' at the end of time.

The language is strange and dream-like, and its scope mindblowing; perhaps that is one reason why we tend to neglect or skirt round the book with some suspicion. We are uneasy because it bypasses our logical faculties, where we tend to feel 'safe', with at least the illusion of understanding and control. Here we are in foreign territory, and meaning does not easily yield itself to the conscious mind. The apocalyptic language cuts right through to our imaginative and intuitive qualities and, through it, we are challenged to allow Christ to stretch our capacity to receive his abundant life.

Short silence

Bidding prayers

Heavenly Father, may we know Christ as the beginning and end of all things.
For you are the Alpha and the Omega, the beginning and the end.

Heavenly Father, may we be open to seeking you through the workings of our unconscious minds.
For you are the Alpha and the Omega, the beginning and the end.

Heavenly Father, may we be honest with you about our fear of the unknown.

For you are the Alpha and the Omega, the beginning and the end.

Heavenly Father, may we see all things in the light of your eternity.

For you are the Alpha and the Omega, the beginning and the end.

Collect

Almighty God,
veiled in dazzling darkness, light invisible,
whose fullness will always exceed our human grasp;
through inspiration of poet and artist
and by the mysterious cyphers of word and image,
point us to the depths of divine reality.
So may our hearts rejoice
and our whole being embrace the One who is,
and who was, and who is to come.
In Jesus' name we pray.
Amen

Trinity 10

Opening prayer

Father of all, help us to trust in you through all the changing weather-patterns that make up the fabric of our lives. May we hold to your love through rain and sunshine, light and shadow, looking to you alone as the rock and constant guide. In Jesus' name we pray. Amen

Reading

Good things and bad, life and death, poverty and wealth, come from the Lord. The Lord's gift remains with the devout, and his favour brings lasting success. One becomes rich through diligence and self-denial, and the reward allotted to him is this: when he says, 'I have found rest, and now I shall feast on my goods!' he does not know how long it will be until he leaves them to others and dies. Stand by your agreement and attend to it, and grow old in your work. Do not wonder at the works of a sinner, but trust in the Lord and keep at your job; for it is easy in the sight of the Lord to make the poor rich suddenly, in an instant.

ECCLESIASTICUS 11:14–21

Reflection

The voice of Ecclesiasticus once more rings out across the centuries, and again we are alerted to its familiar ring. Haven't we read these things before, in other places? 'Good things and bad... poverty and wealth, come from the Lord' (v. 14; see Matthew 5:45); 'The Lord's gift remains with the devout...

lasting success' (v. 15; Psalm 1:1–3); 'I have found… now I shall feast on my goods!' (v. 19; Luke 12:16–21); 'Do not wonder… keep at your job' (v. 21; John 21:21–22); 'Stand by your agreement and attend to it' (v. 20; see Matthew 20:1–16, especially vv. 10–13); 'It is easy in the sight of the Lord to make the poor rich suddenly, in an instant' (v. 21; Job 42:10). There are more: we find within this book a dense network of scriptural resonances and cross-references that will enrich our prayer and meditation.

The exhortation to 'grow old in your work' may strike cruelly on the ears of those whose jobs and livelihoods are under threat, but the underlying message of these words offers a breath of refreshment and relief to all whose lives are restless, weary, fragmented and torn apart by competing duties and desires. Give up the idea that the grass is always greener somewhere else and the unequal struggle to try to stay ahead of the pack. If we cannot find something of God here, in this moment, in this situation, we will find him nowhere else.

Short silence

Bidding prayers

We bring our prayers and concerns to our heavenly Father, whose wisdom transcends all ages.

God of all time, we thank you for all those you have entrusted with your message.
May we trust in the Lord and learn from those who have gone before us.

God of all time, we thank you that you call us from greed and selfishness to generosity and openness of heart.
May we trust in the Lord and learn from those who have gone before us.

God of all time, we thank you that you call us to focus on the beam in our own eye rather than the speck in our neighbour's.
May we trust in the Lord and learn from those who have gone before us.

God of all time, we thank you that you call us from restless striving to stability in your love.
May we trust in the Lord and learn from those who have gone before us.

Collect

God of the ages,
through many and various voices
you speak your wisdom to us through time.
May the words of the wise
be to us an anchor of stability,
a foundation for our prayer
and a flaming pathway
into your living heart of love.
We ask this in Jesus' name.
Amen

Trinity 11

Opening prayer

Almighty God, we pray this day for a will that is quick to do your bidding, and for a heart that is dilated with love and compassion for your world. In Jesus' name we pray. Amen

Reading

When God saw what [the Ninevites] did, how they turned from their evil ways, God changed his mind about the calamity that he had said he would bring upon them; and he did not do it. But this was very displeasing to Jonah, and he became angry... And the Lord said, 'Is it right for you to be angry?' Then Jonah went out of the city and sat down...The Lord appointed a bush...to give shade over his head...so Jonah was very happy about the bush. But when dawn came up the next day, God appointed a worm that attacked the bush, so that it withered. When the sun rose, God prepared a sultry east wind, and the sun beat down on the head of Jonah so that he was faint and... said, 'It is better for me to die than to live.' But God said to Jonah, 'Is it right for you to be angry about the bush?' And he said, 'Yes, angry enough to die.'

JONAH 3:10—4:1, 4–9 (ABRIDGED)

Reflection

The desire to see other people get their 'just deserts' when they have done wrong is a universal human tendency, and not one of our most attractive or appealing characteristics. At

God's instruction, Jonah has been preaching to the people of Nineveh, warning them that they face destruction if they do not repent of their evil ways. When God reprieves the city, however, Jonah feels that his preaching has been rather more successful than the Ninevites deserved.

He is then given a divine lesson in compassion, meticulously planned and structured. 'The Lord appointed a bush…' Jonah sits down in an angry sulk to the east of the city and is very happy for the shelter that the bush gives him from the burning heat. 'God appointed a worm…' The next day at dawn the bush is attacked by a worm, and Jonah's shelter disappears as the bush shrivels up. At sunrise 'God prepared a sultry east wind', which increases Jonah's discomfort in the sweltering heat, and his anger rises to fever pitch at the loss of the bush that gave him shelter.

As God confronts Jonah with his topsy-turvy values and lack of compassion, so he also confronts us. What situations in our own lives trigger our angry self-righteousness? Who, for us, are 'the people of Nineveh' who we feel are not deserving of God's forgiveness?

Short silence

Bidding prayers
In faith and trust, and aware of our weakness, we bring our prayers before almighty God.

Heavenly Father, help us grow in compassion, so that we may rejoice in the mercy you show to others.
You are gracious and merciful, O Lord, and abounding in steadfast love.

Heavenly Father, forgive us when we react with self-righteousness when others fall.
You are gracious and merciful, O Lord, and abounding in steadfast love.

Heavenly Father, make us teachable, so that we may learn your lessons of compassion.
You are gracious and merciful, O Lord, and abounding in steadfast love.

Heavenly Father, may we increasingly come to see ourselves in intricate connection with the whole of your creation.
You are gracious and merciful, O Lord, and abounding in steadfast love.

Collect

Almighty God,
you reach out to your people
with justice and compassion.
When we take the moral high ground
and rejoice in the failings of another,
teach us, with Jonah,
that we too are sinners
in receipt of your forgiveness and love.
We ask this in Jesus' name.
Amen

Trinity 12

Opening prayer

Let the words of my mouth and the meditation of my heart be
acceptable to you, O Lord, my rock and my redeemer. Amen
(Psalm 19:14)

Reading

How great a forest is set ablaze by a small fire! And the
tongue is a fire. The tongue is placed among our members
as a world of iniquity; it stains the whole body, sets on fire
the cycle of nature, and is itself set on fire by hell. For every
species of beast and bird, of reptile and sea creature, can
be tamed and has been tamed by the human species, but
no one can tame the tongue—a restless evil, full of deadly
poison. With it we bless the Lord and Father, and with it we
curse those who are made in the likeness of God. From the
same mouth come blessing and cursing.

JAMES 3:5B–10

Reflection

James' powerful words on the capacity of the tongue for
good and evil are so clear that, on one level, they need very
little unpacking. Benedict, in his fourth-century Rule, wisely
warns his monks, 'Do not grumble or speak ill of others',[13]
and we too will probably have experienced some of the ways
in which thoughtless or hurtful words can damage relationships. So often, we are not even aware that we are speaking
destructively. It was not until the priest and author Stephen
Cherry decided one year to give up grumbling for Lent[14] that

he realised how ingrained the habit had become—and he is not alone!

But there is a deeper level of meaning here. With the reference to creatures of all species, James makes a connection with the account in Genesis where God's word brings the creation into being. As part of that process, humans are created in the likeness of God; and when we speak truthfully and compassionately, we share in the creation of God's kingdom. When we speak untruthfully, we are helping to create a world in opposition to that kingdom.

So, for James, the greatest evil does not lie in grumbling or a passing angry word, damaging though that can be. It is found rather 'in the creation of distorted worlds of meaning within which the word of truth is suppressed'.[15]

Short silence

Bidding prayers

We bring our prayers to our heavenly Father, seeking his guidance that we may use our gift of speech to his glory.

May our speech be used to bless, not curse.
Open our lips, O Lord, and our mouth shall proclaim your praise.

May our speech be used to build up, not destroy.
Open our lips, O Lord, and our mouth shall proclaim your praise.

May our speech be used to praise, not blame.
Open our lips, O Lord, and our mouth shall proclaim your praise.

May our speech be used for truth, not falsehood.
Open our lips, O Lord, and our mouth shall proclaim your praise.

Collect

Almighty God,
you gift us with speech and word,
that we may share in your mission
of truth-bearing in our world.
Help us to reverence the beauty of language,
and may we never forget
its power for good and evil.
We ask this in Jesus' name.
Amen

Trinity 13

Opening prayer

Almighty God, your ways are not our ways, neither are your thoughts our thoughts. Challenge, we pray, the poverty of our vision and the fear that prevents us from seeing the scope of your working in our world. We ask this in Jesus' name. Amen

Reading

Thus says the Lord to his anointed, to Cyrus, whose right hand I have grasped to subdue nations before him and strip kings of their robes, to open doors before him—and the gates shall not be closed: I will go before you and level the mountains, I will break in pieces the doors of bronze and cut through the bars of iron, I will give you the treasures of darkness and riches hidden in secret places, so that you may know that it is I, the Lord, the God of Israel, who call you by your name. For the sake of my servant Jacob, and Israel my chosen, I call you by your name, I surname you, though you do not know me… I arm you, though you do not know me.

ISAIAH 45:1–5 (ABRIDGED)

Reflection

'I am about to do a new thing; now it springs forth, do you not perceive it?' So God speaks through Isaiah (43:19), and in today's passage we see the 'new thing' revealed. Cyrus is called and appointed as God's messiah-deliverer—a crucial instrument in the divine plan to free the Israelites from exile.

But why is this 'new'? The pattern here is a familiar one, echoing God's earlier call and commission of the servant, that enigmatic figure who 'will bring forth justice to the nations' (Isaiah 42:1).

The disturbingly 'new thing' for the chosen people is that Cyrus is a Persian king and not an Israelite, and he does not know the Israelites' God. In this powerful passage, the prophecy makes clear that such ignorance is not a barrier to the furtherance of God's purposes, and that God himself is leading Cyrus to awareness of him by the ways of darkness and unknowing (45:3).

We are likely to develop tunnel-vision if we confine our perception of God's workings to the well-worn and familiar (sometimes overfamiliar) channels. The artificial limitations we try to impose on God will never prevent him from moving through whatever channels he chooses. Isaiah's prophecy challenges the Israelites' insularity; it should prepare us also to see the power of God at work in unexpected people, deepening our vision in ways that may challenge, disturb and delight.

Short silence

Bidding prayers

In confidence and trust we bring our prayers·to God, who sees the treasure hidden in dark and secret places.

Heavenly Father, deepen our awareness of your presence in the places of pain and suffering in our world.
Open our hearts, Lord, to the riches hidden in secret places.

Heavenly Father, deepen our awareness of your presence in all who are working for justice and peace.
Open our hearts, Lord, to the riches hidden in secret places.

Heavenly Father, deepen our awareness of your presence in all who work for the good of our local communities.
Open our hearts, Lord, to the riches hidden in secret places.

Heavenly Father, deepen our awareness of your presence in those parts of our inner selves that we are afraid to reveal to others and to you.
Open our hearts, Lord, to the riches hidden in secret places.

Collect

Almighty God,
you work through friend and foe alike
and your love knows no partiality.
Remove, we pray, the shades from our eyes
and melt the fear in our hearts;
deepen our vision, Father,
that we may rejoice to see your work
in the challenging and the unexpected.
In Jesus' name we pray.
Amen

Trinity 14

Opening prayer

Heavenly Father, give us grace this day to lift our eyes above the cares and pressures of our daily life. In joy and sorrow, need and plenty, may we know your protective and guiding presence, now and always. We ask this for Jesus' sake. Amen

Reading

I lift up my eyes to the hills—from where will my help come? My help comes from the Lord, who made heaven and earth. He will not let your foot be moved; he who keeps you will not slumber. He who keeps Israel will neither slumber nor sleep. The Lord is your keeper; the Lord is your shade at your right hand. The sun shall not strike you by day, nor the moon by night. The Lord will keep you from all evil; he will keep your life. The Lord will keep your going out and your coming in for this time on and for evermore.

PSALM 121

Reflection

After Psalm 23, Psalm 121 is arguably the most familiar and well-loved, and both psalms express very similar beliefs concerning the watchful protectiveness of God. Psalm 121 is the second in a group of 15, each of which is individually titled 'A Song of Ascents', and it is thought that the group may have been used by pilgrims as prayers of celebration and trust while on their way to Jerusalem. Psalm 121 offers a confident and eloquent affirmation of God's providence and protection.

The scale of that protection is all-encompassing: 'The Lord who made heaven and earth' (v. 2) is the same Lord who 'will keep your going out and your coming in' (v. 8). From the mindblowing immensity of the universe to the particular cares and concerns of his people, it is the same God who has compassionate care and concern for all.

Christian history has resonated with the psalm's pilgrimage theme, adopting Psalm 121 as the travellers' psalm. David Livingstone is said to have recited it on the morning of his departure for Africa, and similar protective sentiments are echoed in a number of ancient and contemporary Celtic blessings. In some parts of the church, it has found a place in the baptism liturgy, and it is frequently requested at funeral services. For all Christian people throughout history, it has been a celebration of the journey of life.

Short silence

Bidding prayers

We commit our prayers to God our Father, our abiding and loving protector through the journey of life.

In times of sorrow and despair,
Our help comes from the Lord, who made heaven and earth.

In times of joy and gladness,
Our help comes from the Lord, who made heaven and earth.

In times of doubt and uncertainty,
Our help comes from the Lord, who made heaven and earth.

Through all the changing patterns of life,
Our help comes from the Lord, who made heaven and earth.

Collect

Creator God,
from life's dawn until its ending,
we live and move
in the shadow of your protective love.
In anxiety and tranquillity,
in sorrow and in joy,
may we sense the presence of your shielding hand.
In our journeying and our resting places
may we come to know you,
our loving Father,
and the shepherd and guide of our souls.
For Jesus' sake we pray.
Amen

Trinity 15

Opening prayer

Almighty God, we pray that you would lift us above the tyranny of preening self-congratulation. Help us to know you as the source of all our gifts, and the guiding reality upholding the whole of our life. In Jesus' name we pray. Amen

Reading

If anyone else has reason to be confident in the flesh, I have more: circumcised on the eighth day, a member of the people of Israel, of the tribe of Benjamin, a Hebrew born of Hebrews; as to the law, a Pharisee; as to zeal, a persecutor of the church; as to righteousness under the law, blameless. Yet whatever gains I had, these I have come to regard as loss because of Christ. More than that, I regard everything as loss because of the surpassing value of knowing Christ Jesus my Lord. For his sake I have suffered the loss of all things, and I regard them as rubbish, in order that I may gain Christ and be found in him, not having a righteousness of my own that comes from the law, but one that comes through faith in Christ, the righteousness from God based on faith.

PHILIPPIANS 3:4–9

Reflection

When we apply for a job, much careful effort needs to be put in to submitting a good application. We want to present ourselves in the best possible light, so alongside the usual record of work and educational achievement we also list those extra gifts and accomplishments that may provide 'added value' and help us to stand out from the crowd.

In this passage, Paul lists his own impeccable religious credentials, but there is a twist: he names them not to boast, intimidate or impress others but to show that, despite these advantages, with regard to Christ he still managed to get things completely and utterly *wrong*. As a result, he has come to see that all his gifts and advantages are just so much 'rubbish' and not to be trusted. There is nothing he can claim as his own, apart from Christ.

We too may have gifts and experience that stand us in good stead and would perhaps appeal to a potential employer, but we run into trouble if we become too attached to our own hype. We may start to believe that we actually are better/nicer/smarter than others, and that what gives us some kind of 'edge' is our own cleverness. Like Paul, we may have to learn the hard way that we have no natural entitlement, and that any 'righteousness' we may possess comes not from our own ability or goodness but from Christ alone.

Short silence

Bidding prayers

Let us bring our prayers to God with openness of heart and mind, asking that we may see ourselves as he sees us.

Help us, Lord, to lay aside the masks we present to the world.
Our faith and trust, Lord, are in you alone.

Help us, Lord, to trust in your strength to uphold us.
Our faith and trust, Lord, are in you alone.

Help us, Lord, to know the source of our gifts and talents.
Our faith and trust, Lord, are in you alone.

Help us, Lord, to rejoice in the successes of others.
Our faith and trust, Lord, are in you alone.

Collect

Heavenly Father,
you gift us with varying circumstances
of birth and family, of education and financial means.
Whatever our material situation,
you call each one of us to your service;
help us to look not to our wealth or poverty,
our natural ability or talents,
but to Christ, the giver of all good gifts
and the source and the end of our pilgrimage.
We ask this in his precious name.
Amen

Trinity 16

Opening prayer

*Almighty God, give us the courage, we pray, to defend the weak
and to stand up for what is right. We pray also that we may never
lose sight of the fact that Christ loved the world and its people
so much that he died for their redemption. In his name we pray.
Amen*

Reading

Once when Joshua was near Jericho, he looked up and
saw a man standing before him with a drawn sword in his
hand. Joshua went to him and said to him, 'Are you one
of us, or one of our adversaries?' He replied, 'Neither; but
as commander of the army of the Lord I have now come.'
And Joshua fell on his face to the earth and worshipped,
and he said to him, 'What do you command your servant,
my lord?' The commander of the army of the Lord said to
Joshua, 'Remove the sandals from your feet, for the place
where you stand is holy.' And Joshua did so.

JOSHUA 5:13–15

Reflection

Joshua's encounter with the angel before the battle of Jericho
is strikingly reminiscent of Moses' experience with the burning bush (Exodus 3). In both situations, an angel appears
as God's vanguard, although here Joshua seems initially unaware that the man is a divine messenger. It is only when
the angel declares himself that Joshua prostrates himself in
worship, and the instruction to remove his sandals because

he is on holy ground is identical to the one given to Moses.

The Hebrew Bible's accounts of God's sanction for the Israelite genocide against the Canaanites make for hard reading and offer a terrible moral dilemma for today's Christian sensibilities. The assumption that God is on our side and will give us special protection is a tendency also evident in wars of more recent times. Israel certainly believed passionately that this was so, and it was only very gradually that they began to perceive their calling to be a light to the nations (Isaiah 60:3). When the angel declared that he was not on the side of either the Israelites or their enemies, it must have been startlingly unexpected.

We may well have a keen sense of right and wrong, which may, on different occasions, be either accurate or mistaken. But a growing closeness to God will draw us more deeply into his vision of things, as we realise that we are part of a world where Christ has died for all people, without distinction.

Short silence

Bidding prayers

In trust we bring our prayers to God, who sees the hearts of all his people.

In times of war and civil unrest, may we not forget our common humanity.
Bless us, Lord, for we stand on holy ground.

In times of injustice and inequality, may we not forget our common humanity.
Bless us, Lord, for we stand on holy ground.

In times of personal comfort and ease, may we not forget our common humanity.
Bless us, Lord, for we stand on holy ground.

In times of plenty, with more than we need, may we not forget our common humanity.
Bless us, Lord, for we stand on holy ground.

Collect

Almighty God,
you call all people to yourself
within the loving embrace of your Son.
When we are tempted to deny the humanity of others,
temper our inhumanity;
and may we know that,
whatever the cause of our enmity,
we are equally part of the world
that Christ loves
and for which he died.
In Jesus' name we pray.
Amen

Trinity 17

Opening prayer

Heavenly Father, amid the delight and sorrow of this beautiful world, we are a pilgrim people. We thank you for the gift of our life and the mingled joy and pain it encompasses. Help us, we pray, to accept that here we have no lasting city and to keep our eyes on you, the source and end of all our journeying. Amen

Reading

By the rivers of Babylon—there we sat down and there we wept when we remembered Zion. On the willows there we hung up our harps. For there our captors asked us for songs, and our tormentors asked for mirth, saying, 'Sing us one of the songs of Zion!' How could we sing the Lord's song in a foreign land? If I forget you, O Jerusalem, let my right hand wither! Let my tongue cling to the roof of my mouth, if I do not remember you, if I do not set Jerusalem above my highest joy.

PSALM 137:1–6

Reflection

The sheer passion of these words leaps off the page with an immediacy that hits us between the eyes. Almost certainly written during the Babylonian exile of 587–539BC, they are painful evidence of the grief and disorientation of the Israelite people. Yet there is more being expressed here than simply the loss of home and country. The people's grief has its roots in a far deeper anguish—the belief that, in losing the land, they have also lost the God who gave it to them. To worship God in an alien land was (so they believed) impossible (v. 4), and their relationship with him had to be slowly and painfully rediscovered.

It is an experience that many have shared in the centuries since. Recently I met a woman in her mid-50s who, as a ten-year-old, had emigrated to Australia with her family. A warm and trusting childhood faith was severely shaken as she tried to replant her spiritual roots in what felt like an alien country. It was only when she discovered aboriginal culture, with its belief in the sacredness of the land, that her sense of relationship and belonging was rekindled.

Maybe such experiences—the ancient and the contemporary —serve to remind us that we are all exiles on earth. We shield ourselves from this reality with material security; but, when that security is stripped away, we are challenged to allow our vision of God to be expanded.

Short silence

Bidding prayers

We bring our prayers to the God who, whatever life may bring, will never leave us.

Lord, in times of stress and insecurity,
Teach us to sing your song in a strange land.

Lord, in situations of strangeness and unfamiliarity,
Teach us to sing your song in a strange land.

Lord, in times of sorrow and loss,
Teach us to sing your song in a strange land.

Lord, when our image of you is too small,
Teach us to sing your song in a strange land.

Collect

Lord God our Father,
on our journey through this life
we are exiles in a world not our own.
As we relish its beauty
and share in its pain,
clarify and strengthen our inner vision,
that we may increasingly know
that in all our living
we are breathing the clear air of your kingdom,
which is our true home.
We ask this for Jesus' sake.
Amen

Trinity 18

Opening prayer

Heavenly Father, we pray for honesty in our relationships with you and with others. Help us to subject our motives and attitudes to the clear light of your scrutiny, that we may worship you in spirit and in truth. We ask this in Jesus' name. Amen

Reading

[Jesus] also told this parable to some who trusted in themselves that they were righteous and regarded others with contempt: 'Two men went up to the temple to pray, one a Pharisee and the other a tax collector. The Pharisee, standing by himself, was praying thus, "God, I thank you that I am not like other people: thieves, rogues, adulterers, or even like this tax collector. I fast twice a week; I give a tenth of all my income." But the tax collector, standing far off, would not even look up to heaven, but was beating his breast and saying, 'God, be merciful to me, a sinner!' I tell you, this man went down to his home justified rather than the other; for all who exalt themselves will be humbled, but all who humble themselves will be exalted.'

LUKE 18:9–14

Reflection

The parable that forms today's reading appears to need very little explanation. Isn't it self-explanatory? What further elaboration does it need? The introductory words explain exactly what the parable is about. It is also true, though, that familiarity can breed contempt, and the fact that we think we know what something is all about may be an indication that we need to examine it a little more closely.

We think we know what the parable says because the behaviour of both the Pharisee and the tax collector are so vividly drawn—the Pharisee strident in his bragging superiority, the tax collector the epitome of submissive humility. Our problem of non-recognition arises because our own leanings towards self-aggrandisement tend to be more subtle than those of the Pharisee, so we do not recognise them for what they really are. We may present a mask of apparent humility to the world, while at the same time secretly nursing a belief in our own innate superiority to others—and perhaps the most damaging area where this can happen is in our spiritual life.

I once heard of a priest who preached on this parable. Climbing into the pulpit, he smiled at the congregation and said, 'Hands up anyone who didn't think, "Thank God I'm not like that Pharisee!"' And then he returned to his seat…

Short silence

Bidding prayers

Knowing our frailty and our kinship with all people, in trust and hope we bring our prayers to God our Father.

Forgive us, heavenly Father, when we boost our self-esteem at the expense of others.
Lord, hear our prayer: we have all sinned and fallen short of your glory.

Forgive us, heavenly Father, when our competitive instinct leads to the diminishment of others.
Lord, hear our prayer: we have all sinned and fallen short of your glory.

Help us, heavenly Father, to see others as you see them.
Lord, hear our prayer: we have all sinned and fallen short of your glory.

Help us, heavenly Father, to see ourselves as you see us.
Lord, hear our prayer: we have all sinned and fallen short of your glory.

Collect

Almighty God,
against the measure of your justice
we have all sinned
and fallen short of your glory.
As we journey through life,
deepen our sense of this truth;
help us to see that we are one with our brothers and sisters,
and that we are all alike
in need of your mercy and forgiveness.
In Jesus' name we pray.
Amen

Trinity 19

Opening prayer

Almighty God, quicken our hearts, we pray, to your presence among us. Help us to be alert to the promptings of your Spirit, that all our living this day may be in tune with the life of your kingdom. Amen

Reading

Be careful then how you live, not as unwise people but as wise, making the most of the time, because the days are evil. So do not be foolish, but understand what the will of the Lord is. Do not get drunk with wine, for that is debauchery; but be filled with the Spirit, as you sing psalms and hymns and spiritual songs among yourselves, singing and making melody to the Lord in your hearts, giving thanks to God the Father at all times and for everything in the name of our Lord Jesus Christ. Be subject to one another out of reverence for Christ.

EPHESIANS 5:15–21

Reflection

The exhortation to choose to live wisely has ancient scriptural roots. The Old Testament is punctuated with such instruction, which formed part of the wisdom tradition (Deuteronomy 30:15–20; Psalm 1; Proverbs 4:10–14), and it resonates also with Jesus' eschatological teaching regarding the need for wise action in readiness for the coming of the Son of Man (Luke 12:35–48; Matthew 25:1–13). Evils were thought to increase as the world moved towards its end, making the question of how people should wisely 'make the most of the time' a matter of urgency.

We may not know the day or the hour (Mark 13:32), but the advice offered here holds true in any generation. Precisely because we do not know the time, this teaching is always fresh. It offers guidance for living, not only because we do not know when the end will come but because it also provides a framework for a sustainable, peaceful and cohesive community life, centred on Christ.

Perhaps the key is to be found in verses 18–20 ('Be filled with the Spirit...'). As we go about our daily lives we are encouraged to 'practise the presence of God' in such a way that submission to one another becomes natural. Centred in Christ and in the clear light of the Spirit, prayer becomes as instinctive as breathing, and all our living becomes subject to the guidance of that inspiration.

Short silence

Bidding prayers

In praise and thankfulness we bring our prayers to our heavenly Father.

We pray for wisdom in the decisions we must make today.
Father, we thank you for everything, in the name of our Lord Jesus Christ.

We pray for compassion in the suffering we will witness today.
Father, we thank you for everything, in the name of our Lord Jesus Christ.

We pray that we will reverence the people we will meet today.
Father, we thank you for everything, in the name of our Lord Jesus Christ.

We pray for grateful hearts in all we will experience today.
Father, we thank you for everything, in the name of our Lord Jesus Christ.

Collect

Heavenly Father,
you call us with urgency
to centre our lives and relationships
on the foundation that is Christ.
In the power of the Spirit,
may we relish the time you give us
with gratitude in our hearts;
and in all our living may we know your presence,
illuminating each moment
with the light of your kingdom.
In Jesus' name we pray.
Amen

Trinity 20

Opening prayer

Holy God, we pray today for the grace to be open and receptive to the renewing, transforming power of the Spirit within us. We ask this in Jesus' name. Amen

Reading

I appeal to you therefore, brothers and sisters, by the mercies of God, to present your bodies as a living sacrifice, holy and acceptable to God, which is your spiritual worship. Do not be conformed to this world, but be transformed by the renewing of your minds, so that you may discern what is the will of God—what is good and acceptable and perfect.

ROMANS 12:1–2

Reflection

How are we to live truthfully, at peace within our communities and with ourselves? It is not enough for us to strive to live authentically by a sheer effort of human will, however good and honourable our intentions. Paul knows only too well the sinful capacity of the human mind and its potential for manipulation of others in accordance with its own, often unconscious motives.

Yet there is no dualism intended here: Paul's instructions for life in Christian communities are no less relevant for the believer's relationship with the world outside those communities. We are not being urged to a holier-than-thou retreat into some disembodied and unsullied spiritual realm; the concern is rather about right thinking and action in the world and within relationships. For Paul, the renewed mind is one in which the inner compass is attracted and compelled by the beauty of the holy rather than by the demands of the ego. Where this happens, the process of discernment will naturally tend towards the will of God.

What is needed is nothing less than a complete transformation of the mind from within by the power of God. Such a process requires an attitude of receptivity on our part and a willingness to invite the healing, renewing power of God to work in the dusty and often dark recesses of our selves.

Short silence

Bidding prayers

We bring our prayers to our holy God, who alone can bring healing and renewal to our souls.

Merciful God, clarify our vision, so that we may see the world through your eyes.
Transform us, Lord, we pray, by the renewing of our minds.

Merciful God, sharpen our insight, so that we may see and love Christ in our neighbour.
Transform us, Lord, we pray, by the renewing of our minds.

Merciful God, deepen our compassion, so that we may reach out to those in pain.
Transform us, Lord, we pray, by the renewing of our minds.

Merciful God, calm our fears, so that we may be open to your healing and transforming power in our lives.
Transform us, Lord, we pray, by the renewing of our minds.

Collect

Holy God,
you call us to see the world as you see it
through the transformation
and renewal of our minds.
Lighten our inner darkness, we pray,
and make us receptive
to the probing, healing work
of our divine Physician.
We ask this in Jesus' name.
Amen

Trinity 21

Opening prayer

Almighty God, in our work today we pray you would release us from unhealthy competition. Give us a realistic appraisal of our abilities, that we may, with peace and joy, discover our place within your body. We ask this in Jesus' name. Amen

Reading

For by the grace given to me I say to everyone among you not to think of yourself more highly than you ought to think, but to think with sober judgment, each according to the measure of faith that God has assigned. For as in one body we have many members, and not all the members have the same function, so we, who are many, are one body in Christ... We have gifts that differ according to the grace given to us: prophecy, in proportion to faith; ministry, in ministering; the teacher, in teaching; the exhorter, in exhortation; the giver, in generosity; the leader, in diligence; the compassionate, in cheerfulness. Let love be genuine; hate what is evil, hold fast to what is good; love one another with mutual affection; outdo one another in showing honour.

ROMANS 12:3–10

Reflection

We begin where last week's passage ended, as Paul continues to explore some of the implications of a mind transformed in Christ, in terms of ministry and relationships within the Christian community. In urging believers not to think more highly of themselves than they ought (v. 3), Paul first warns against the kind of striving that could cause those who are mistakenly motivated to overreach themselves. The assumption is that those whose minds are renewed and transformed in Christ (v. 2) should be able to view themselves and their abilities with a degree of objectivity and realism. A mind possessing 'sober judgment', able to acknowledge but not overestimate its capacity, will make a healthy contribution to the good of the body more easily than one driven by pride and personal ambition.

Just as Paul alerts us to the danger of an exaggerated sense of our own giftedness, so he implicitly warns against an *under*estimation of our abilities. False modesty can be as crippling as no modesty at all, as both extremes focus an unhealthy attention on the individual and their self-perception. 'Let love be genuine,' urges Paul; 'love one another with mutual affection' (vv. 9–10). If competition there must be, let it be directed outwards, in attitudes of honour and mutual respect.

Short silence

Bidding prayers

In humility and thanksgiving we bring our prayers to God, who equips us to work together for the good of his kingdom.

We seek your help, O Lord, in those times when our pride gets the better of us.
By the grace of God, may we hold fast to what is good.

We seek your help, O Lord, in those times when false modesty cripples us.
By the grace of God, may we hold fast to what is good.

We seek your help, O God, in those times when we look to others for reassurance rather than to you.
By the grace of God, may we hold fast to what is good.

We seek your help, O God, to grow in that 'sober judgment' which sees ourselves as you see us.
By the grace of God, may we hold fast to what is good.

Collect

Heavenly Father,
you call us as members of your body
and equip us with varieties of gifts.
May our love for one another be genuine,
and give us the judgment to know our place
within the kaleidoscopic patterning
of your kingdom.
In Jesus' name we pray.
Amen

Trinity 22

Opening prayer

Lord God, when we are tired and hard-pressed, help us to look to you for renewal and seek your presence within unwelcome situations. For Jesus' sake we pray. Amen

Reading

From there he set out and went away to the region of Tyre. He entered a house and did not want anyone to know he was there. Yet he could not escape notice, but a woman whose little daughter had an unclean spirit immediately heard about him, and she came and bowed down at his feet. Now the woman was a Gentile, of Syrophoenician origin. She begged him to cast the demon out of her daughter. He said to her, 'Let the children be fed first, for it is not fair to take the children's food and throw it to the dogs.' But she answered him, 'Sir, even the dogs under the table eat the children's crumbs.' Then he said to her, 'For saying that, you may go—the demon has left your daughter.' So she went home, found the child lying on the bed, and the demon gone.

MARK 7:24–30

Reflection

What is going on here? Why does Jesus treat this anguished woman so harshly?

It is important to remind ourselves that Jesus, while Son of God, was also fully human. He got hungry, thirsty and tired; he wept at the death of his friend; he experienced great suffering and mental anguish; he gave and received love. There are also signs (dare we say it?) that at times he displayed a very human irritation (see Luke 2:49–50; John 2:4; Mark 11:12–14), and it may be that this incident took place at another of those times. For some time before this, Jesus has been attempting to get the disciples away for some rest, but people and their relentless needs follow them everywhere. Jesus' hope for a brief period of anonymity (v. 24) is abruptly shattered by the arrival of this Gentile woman, and he responds to her request sharply and dismissively.

But the woman's reply ricochets back, stopping Jesus in his tracks. Irritation turns to admiration, and he attributes the subsequent healing not to her great faith but to her sharp and witty reply to his rebuke. She is clearly a woman who, despite her distress, is not going to be easily cowed. Concerned though Jesus may be that his mission should be to Israel rather than to the Gentiles (see Matthew 15:24), his personal compassion for the woman wins through as she engages him on his own verbal terms.

Short silence

Bidding prayers

We bring our prayers and concerns to God, who urges us never to lose heart.

When our prayer feels dry and uninspired, we seek your wider vision.
When we are discouraged, Lord, may we never give up hope.

When our patience runs short, we seek your deeper understanding.

When we are discouraged, Lord, may we never give up hope.

When our generosity dries up, we seek your greater compassion.

When we are discouraged, Lord, may we never give up hope.

When our strength is exhausted, we seek your divine renewal.

When we are discouraged, Lord, may we never give up hope.

Collect

Heavenly Father,
in a life of constant giving,
your Son knew hunger and thirst
and the need for rest and refreshment.
When we feel we have nothing left to give,
help us to trust
in your healing powers of renewal
and to know that, in you,
we have all we need
to fulfil our part
in your purposes for the world.
In Jesus' name we pray.
Amen

Last Sunday after Trinity

Opening prayer

Heavenly Father, we pray this day for the gift of an open and humble heart, and ask that we may welcome everyone we meet with equal warmth and generosity. We ask this in Jesus' name. Amen

Reading

On one occasion… Jesus was going to the house of a leader of the Pharisees to eat a meal on the sabbath… When he noticed how the guests chose the places of honour, he told them a parable. 'When you are invited by someone to a wedding banquet, do not sit down at the place of honour, in case someone more distinguished than you has been invited… For all who exalt themselves will be humbled, and those who humble themselves will be exalted.' He said also to the one who had invited him, 'When you give a luncheon or a dinner, do not invite your friends or your brothers or your relatives or rich neighbours, in case they may invite you in return, and you would be repaid. But when you give a banquet, invite the poor, the crippled, the lame, and the blind. And you will be blessed, because they cannot repay you, for you will be repaid at the resurrection of the righteous.'

LUKE 14:1, 7–8, 11–14 (ABRIDGED)

Reflection

In the ancient Middle East, meals were important social cere-monies. Deeply important issues like who one ate with and where one was asked to sit were clear indicators of where a person ranked in the social hierarchy. Here, Jesus is a guest at a sabbath meal given by 'a leader of the Pharisees' (v. 1), and immediately the gulf between the approaches of host and guest is laid bare.

Jesus challenges the assumptions of the other guests and the host. Guests are rebuked for taking the places of honour and urged to hold back, if only to avoid the embarrassment of being asked to move to a lower place. The host is challenged to extend his highly selective invitation list to include those who will never be in a position to repay his hospitality.

Even the eschatological dimension can be governed by self-interest if we believe we will be repaid for our generosity 'at the resurrection of the righteous' (v. 14). The challenges of this chapter take the form of lessons in humility and generosity: ultimately, whether as 'host' or 'guest', we are pointed beyond the thorny issue of self-interest altogether. Our preoccupation with hierarchy and status and where we stand in the pecking order is continually subverted by Jesus and the values he teaches—the values of God's kingdom, where all are equally invited, regardless of social standing, gender, race or creed.

Short silence

Bidding prayers

Our loving Father invites us to his banquet. Let us bring our prayers to him in humility and trust.

We pray for the humility to put others before ourselves.
For all who exalt themselves will be humbled, and those who humble themselves will be exalted.

We pray for generous and welcoming hearts.
For all who exalt themselves will be humbled, and those who humble themselves will be exalted.

We pray that we may serve without looking for personal reward.
For all who exalt themselves will be humbled, and those who humble themselves will be exalted.

We pray for the coming of your kingdom.
For all who exalt themselves will be humbled, and those who humble themselves will be exalted.

Collect

Almighty God,
teach us to be open-hearted hosts
and grateful guests,
looking for no reward
other than the satisfaction
of sharing in the work of your kingdom.
In Jesus' name we pray.
Amen

Fourth Sunday before Advent

Opening prayer

Holy God, we seek your gift of wisdom, to think rightly and act justly in every situation that comes our way. Deepen our listening, that we may discern your wisdom at work in every aspect of your creation. In Jesus' name we pray. Amen

Reading

Wisdom is radiant and unfading, and she is easily discerned by those who love her, and is found by those who seek her. She hastens to make herself known to those who desire her. One who rises early to seek her will have no difficulty, for she will be found sitting at the gate. To fix one's thought on her is perfect understanding, and one who is vigilant on her account will soon be free from care, because she goes about seeking those worthy of her, and she graciously appears to them in their paths, and meets them in every thought.

WISDOM OF SOLOMON 6:12–16

Reflection

This lovely passage from the apocryphal book The Wisdom of Solomon follows the biblical convention of personifying the quality of wisdom. The author here is freely adapting the characterisation found in the book of Proverbs (8:1–17) and introduces it at this point in anticipation of the second part of the book, which focuses on David's son Solomon, a king renowned for his wisdom.

The meaning of wisdom tends to shift and change its shape, according to time and context. As in today's passage, its personification tends to be female. The term is sometimes applied practically to those who have some form of technical skill (Exodus 31:3; Ezekiel 27:8–9) and to those with the ability to make sound and moral decisions (1 Kings 3:9, 12), but it is also used more enigmatically to describe deep mysteries that are hidden from humanity but apparent to God (Proverbs 8:22–31). Wisdom in her fullest sense belongs to God alone.

Our passage beautifully describes the finding-and-being-found paradox that links the believer and God/wisdom. Believers are urged to seek wisdom earnestly—to rise early, to be watchful and to fix their thoughts on her (vv. 14–15). Wisdom responds with reciprocal movement: to those who desire her, 'she hastens to make herself known' (v. 13); 'she will be found sitting at the gate' (v. 14); and to those who seek her 'she graciously appears to them in their paths and meets them in every thought' (v. 16).

Short silence

Bidding prayers

We bring our prayers to our heavenly Father, the Lord of all wisdom.

For those who minister in your Church, in whatever capacity.
Speak, Lord, for those who seek your wisdom will not be disappointed.

For those who work as peacemakers in the troubled areas of our world.
Speak, Lord, for those who seek your wisdom will not be disappointed.

For those who work as peacemakers in the towns and cities
of our country.
**Speak, Lord, for those who seek your wisdom will not be
disappointed.**

For those who work with the sick and dying.
**Speak, Lord, for those who seek your wisdom will not be
disappointed.**

Collect

Creator God,
with you is wisdom
in all her richness and unfading radiance.
Engage our hearts and enlighten our minds
with the wisdom that delights
to share with you in the work of creation;
and may we diligently seek wisdom this day
in every thought
and in every situation and encounter,
to the glory of your name.
Through Jesus Christ our Lord.
Amen

Third Sunday before Advent

Opening prayer

Holy God, in all the activity that will carry us along today, help us to wait upon you in the silence of our souls. Amen

Reading

For God alone my soul waits in silence; from him comes my salvation. He alone is my rock and my salvation, my fortress; I shall never be shaken. How long will you assail a person, will you batter your victim, all of you, as you would a leaning wall, a tottering fence? … They take pleasure in falsehood; they bless with their mouths, but inwardly they curse. For God alone my soul waits in silence, for my hope is from him… Trust in him at all times, O people; pour out your heart before him; God is a refuge for us… Put no confidence in extortion, and set no vain hopes on robbery; if riches increase, do not set your heart on them.

PSALM 62:1–5, 8–10

Reflection

'Trust in him at all times, O people' (v. 8). God's reign is breaking into the old world order, bringing new priorities and values. As elsewhere in the Old Testament, the writer confronts his audience with a choice. The old order is marked by violence and deceit, robbery and extortion (vv. 3–4, 9–10) and it carries with it a seductive compulsion. Why not trust our own resources? Why not use our own astuteness to try to improve our position in life? But the priorities of the new order are clear, and they come from God alone, not our own ingenuity. He only is the one for whom the psalmist's soul waits in silence (vv. 1, 5), the rock who will never be shaken (v. 2).

The psalmist's plea for the people to trust in God reaches down to us through the corridors of history. It faces us with questions as pertinent today as ever. Whom do we trust? Where do our deepest loyalties lie? In what, or to whom, do we look for security?

Amid all the questioning, one phrase repeats: 'For God alone my soul waits in silence.' In all the complexity and confusion of today's world, we desperately need to wait silently on God in prayer, listening intently for the still, small voice within. In his strength and with his guidance, we are enabled to navigate a safe pathway.

Short silence

Bidding prayers

In the midst of our busyness and uncertainty, we bring our prayers to God, who always waits within the deep silence of our souls.

Save us from ourselves, Lord, when we seek the approval of others.
For you alone, O Lord, my soul in silence waits.

Save us from ourselves, Lord, when we hide from you in overactivity.
For you alone, O Lord, my soul in silence waits.

Save us from ourselves, Lord, when we forget to listen in our prayer.
For you alone, O Lord, my soul in silence waits.

Save us from ourselves, Lord, when we are blind to the beauties of your world.
For you alone, O Lord, my soul in silence waits.

Collect

Holy God,
our wisdom and our joy,
amid the noise and confusion that surround us,
draw us deep into the heart of your silence.
Enfolded in your love,
may we listen for your still, small voice
speaking peace amid our turmoil
and hope within our hearts.
In Jesus' name we pray.
Amen

Second Sunday before Advent

Opening prayer

Heavenly Lord, in a world seemingly gripped by the inevitability of war and the random unpredictability of natural disaster, help us this day to plant our feet firmly on the rock that is Christ. In his name we pray. Amen

Reading

As [Jesus] came out of the temple, one of his disciples said to him, 'Look, Teacher, what large stones and what large buildings!' Then Jesus asked him, 'Do you see these great buildings? Not one stone will be left here upon another; all will be thrown down... When you hear of wars and rumours of wars, do not be alarmed; this must take place, but the end is still to come. For nation will rise against nation, and kingdom against kingdom; there will be earthquakes in various places; there will be famines. This is but the beginning of the birth pangs.'

MARK 13:1–2, 7–8

Reflection

Since the time of Jesus until the present day, there has never been an age that has not seen within itself the signs of the end of the world. As I was writing this, the latest confident prediction was for 21 May 2011! But when the disciples urge Jesus to tell them when the things he is predicting will come to pass, he warns them not to be tempted to try to fix dates: 'The end is still to come... This is but the beginning of the birth pangs' (vv. 7, 8).

The reality is that all ages manifest their version of the signs indicated by Jesus; all ages experience the beginning of the birth pangs. But this is far from being a mandate for complacency: the task of the disciple is to 'keep awake… for you do not know on what day your Lord is coming' (Matthew 24:42). The disciple's one concern should be to continue to witness to the gospel, however difficult the circumstances (Mark 13:3–13).

Today, people tend to think of prophecy almost exclusively in terms of predicting the future, but we misunderstand if we think this is its primary role. Biblical prophecy, whether in Old or New Testament, was chiefly addressed to the contemporary situation and the probable consequences that would follow if that situation was not rectified. The aim of prophecy was repentance and reform; disaster followed only if the warnings were ignored (compare Jonah 3:10).

Short silence

Bidding prayers

We bring our prayers to our loving Father, seeking his strength and reassurance.

When war gives way to more war, and good people's voices are silenced,
Raise our eyes to you, Lord God, who transcends all time.

When evil appears to get the upper hand,
Raise our eyes to you, Lord God, who transcends all time.

When we cannot see a way out of our present difficulties,
Raise our eyes to you, Lord God, who transcends all time.

When we are tempted to lose hope,
Raise our eyes to you, Lord God, who transcends all time.

Collect

Almighty God,
as from time immemorial,
we live in a world where there are wars
and rumours of wars.
Within the turbulence of this present time,
keep our eyes fixed
on the one true reality:
Christ of the ages,
whose love embraces
and transcends all time,
bringing all things to completion in him.
Amen

Christ the King
(Sunday Next before Advent)

Opening prayer

Heavenly Father, we celebrate today the glorious reality of Christ and his kingdom. As we bow before him in worship and thanksgiving, we pray for the willingness to work with you for the coming of Christ's kingdom on earth, as it is in heaven. Amen

Reading

One of the criminals who were hanged there kept deriding him and saying, 'Are you not the Messiah? Save yourself and us!' But the other rebuked him, saying, 'Do you not fear God, since you are under the same sentence of condemnation? And we indeed have been condemned justly… but this man has done nothing wrong.' Then he said, 'Jesus, remember me when you come into your kingdom.' He replied, 'Truly I tell you, today you will be with me in Paradise.'

LUKE 23:39–43 (ABRIDGED)

Reflection

We stand today on the threshold of Advent, when we will look forward again to the celebration of Christ's coming into our world. As we ready ourselves to enter that time of preparation, let us pause today and reflect on the kingship of Christ, and the kind of kingdom he is bringing in. We must not let our familiarity with the Gospel narratives blunt our minds and hearts to a shocking truth—that on every level, Christ's kingdom is on a collision course with the kingdoms of this world.

The penitent thief in today's reading has lived his life so far by the values of this world. Driven by need or greed, he has taken for himself some of the wealth he has seen others enjoy, and he is paying the penalty his society decrees. But in these moments of agony, he is suddenly overwhelmed by the innocence of Jesus seen alongside his own sin. In the dying Jesus he catches a glimpse of undreamed-of possibilities: a kingdom of love and acceptance, of justice, healing and forgiveness.

With a huge leap of faith, the man reaches out for that which he has fleetingly glimpsed. Jesus' response is instant, with no weighing up of the past: 'Today, you will be with me in Paradise.'

Short silence

Bidding prayers

We come before God in humility and trust as we seek to live the values of his kingdom in our daily lives.

Reigning Lord, we live in a world of great inequality, where the rich get richer and the poor poorer. At times we are complacent and fail to strive for justice.
Forgive us, Lord, and help us to live in the truth of your kingdom.

Reigning Lord, you call us to be beacons of light in a world crying out for your love. Strengthen our desire to reach out to those in pain and to share the blessings we have received.

Forgive us, Lord, and help us to live in the truth of your kingdom.

Reigning Lord, so often we find it difficult to acknowledge our frailty and weakness, hitting out defensively at those whose goodness causes us discomfort.

Forgive us, Lord, and help us to live in the truth of your kingdom.

Reigning Lord, alert us to that small part of the great task that is ours to do, so that we may share in the fulfilment of your purposes for the world.

Forgive us, Lord, and help us to live in the truth of your kingdom.

Collect

Lord Jesus Christ,
whose kingdom is not of this world,
when our pride and fear lead us to collude
with the world's greed and aggression,
inflame our hearts anew with passion and yearning
for the values of your kingdom.
May we journey through this world
in peace and integrity,
and with a thirst for justice for all your creation.
We ask this in your precious name.
Amen

Red Letter Days

John the Evangelist
(27 December)

Opening prayer

*Heavenly Father, set our spirits free and give us wings like eagles,
so that we may plumb the heights and depths of the love you have
for us in your Son, Jesus Christ our Lord. Amen*

Reading

Peter turned and saw the disciple whom Jesus loved following them; he was the one who had reclined next to Jesus
at the supper and had said, 'Lord, who is it that is going
to betray you? … This is the disciple who is testifying to
these things and has written them, and we know that his
testimony is true.

JOHN 21:20, 24

Reflection

The illustrated page introducing John in the Lindisfarne
Gospels shows the evangelist pointing the reader to the scroll
of his Gospel, an eagle soaring aloft behind him. The use of
the eagle as a symbol for John is an ancient one, inspired by
the beginning of his Gospel with its transcending of earth
and time, and the coming of Christ from within the heart of
the divine mystery.

Today's text describes an incident relating to both Peter
and John, and commentators have sometimes seen them as
male versions of Mary and Martha: Peter the man of action,
John the contemplative. Yet this distinction is perhaps too

simplistic. John the beloved disciple, who reclined on Jesus' breast, 'listening to the heartbeat of God' as the Celtic tradition has it, was nevertheless also a man of passion and ardent temperament (John and his brother James were nicknamed 'sons of thunder' by Jesus).

John was a privileged witness of many key events in Jesus' ministry, and at the crucifixion Jesus gave him the care of his mother. Yet John is always more concerned with the depths of the divine mystery concealed within, rather than simply with the events themselves. With John, we too are encouraged to penetrate the contemplative depths and to seek the God who is present in all life.

Short silence

Bidding prayers

We bring our prayers and praise to God, who reaches out to us in love from beyond the boundaries of time and space.

In the midst of the storms and trials of life, we pray that you would gift us with your courage and fearlessness.
May we know ourselves to be at one with you and all creation.

In the midst of the joys and sorrows of life, we pray that you would gift us with your understanding and compassion.
May we know ourselves to be at one with you and all creation.

In the midst of the complexities and confusions of life, we pray that you would gift us with your wisdom and insight.
May we know ourselves to be at one with you and all creation.

In the midst of the trivia and superficialities of life, we pray that you would gift us with a depth of inner vision.
May we know ourselves to be at one with you and all creation.

Collect

Almighty God,
you gave Christ's beloved disciple a contemplative heart,
that he might point us
to the depths of the divine mystery.
Inspire us, we pray,
with his courage and inner vision,
that with our whole being
we may know the richness of your life
at the heart of all creation.
In Jesus' name we pray.
Amen

The Holy Innocents
(28 December)

Opening prayer

Heavenly Father, help us to see Christ in the weak and powerless of this world. May we remember our common humanity with all people, and may our hands be open in welcome. In striving for your justice, help us to work with love and compassion for all your children. Amen

Reading

An angel of the Lord appeared to Joseph in a dream and said, 'Get up, take the child and his mother, and flee to Egypt, and remain there until I tell you; for Herod is about to search for the child, to destroy him.' Then Joseph got up, took the child and his mother by night, and went to Egypt, and remained there until the death of Herod... When Herod saw that he had been tricked by the wise men, he was infuriated, and he sent and killed all the children in and around Bethlehem who were two years old or under, according to the time that he had learned from the wise men.

MATTHEW 2:13–16 (ABRIDGED)

Reflection

Today's reading stuns us with its horror, coming like a shock of cold water to those of us who might prefer to stay with the cosily familiar nativity narratives. King Herod hears from the wise men that a new king of the Jews has been born. Paranoid and fearful for the security of his throne, he can think only of obliterating the threat, and so commits an act of unspeakable cruelty.

How must Mary have felt? Bewilderment, surely, and a sickening fear for her child, so awesomely spoken of, who was suddenly in such danger. Then there was the urgent anxiety of Joseph, the hurried packing of their few belongings, the hurried escape by night and the long, long trek to Egypt and safety.

A few Christmases ago, Merseyside produced *A Liverpool Nativity*, an ambitious community drama. It included hundreds of local people, not only as audience but also as crowds complicit in the action. When Gabriel urged Joseph to take his family and flee to Egypt, the family set out on their journey and the crowd parted to make way for them. Gabriel sent them on their way, movingly urging the crowd, 'Welcome them into your own communities.' In today's world of refugees and suffering children, how open-hearted is our welcome?

Short silence

Bidding prayers

As we pray for the homeless and suffering of our world, we turn to Christ in penitence and hope.

Friend of the friendless, we pray for those who feel they have no one to turn to; show us how we may be channels of your love.
Open our ears, Lord, to the cries of the poor.

Father and mother of the orphan, we pray for those who have no earthly family; show us how we may be channels of your love.

Open our ears, Lord, to the cries of the poor.

Healer of the sick, we pray for those whose lives have been broken by illness of mind, body or spirit; show us how we may be channels of your love.

Open our ears, Lord, to the cries of the poor.

Shelter of the homeless, we pray for those without homes and whose family roots have been destroyed; show us how we may be channels of your love.

Open our ears, Lord, to the cries of the poor.

Collect

Heavenly Father,
your compassionate heart cries out as,
two thousand years on,
children still suffer and refugees
still wander the face of the earth.
Stir our hearts
to generous response,
that little ones may be loved and protected
and refugees may know the security of home.
Through Jesus Christ our Lord.
Amen

The Naming and Circumcision of Jesus (1 January)

Opening prayer

Gracious Father, we thank you that in your Son Jesus Christ you reach out to us in love and call us by name. May our hearts be lifted to you in free and willing response, and may we experience the confidence and joy that comes from knowing that we are your children. Amen

Reading

The shepherds returned, glorifying and praising God for all they had heard and seen, as it had been told them. After eight days had passed, it was time to circumcise the child; and he was called Jesus, the name given by the angel before he was conceived in the womb.

LUKE 2:20–21

Reflection

Eight days after Jesus' birth and the visit of the shepherds come the first two vital elements in the requirements of the law: the circumcision and the naming of Jesus (for the third, see Candlemas below). In line with ancient tradition, the circumcision took place on the eighth day after birth (Genesis 17:12; Leviticus 12:3), and it marked the acceptance of Jesus into the covenant community of Israel.

Luke's emphasis here, though, is not so much on the circumcision as on the naming of the child. In the ancient world, the name did far more than simply distinguish one person from another. It was believed to be a title bearing sacred significance, carrying something of the nature of the person owning it. The name of the deity was believed to be inseparable from his divinity, embodying within it all the deity's character and powers. The special name of the God of Israel, Yahweh, was considered so sacred that general use of it was forbidden. In Exodus 23:21, the name of God is synonymous with his presence.

Luke makes it clear that Jesus had been named not by Joseph but by the angel. In declaring Jesus' future role as the Saviour of his people, his name served as both prophecy and fulfilment.

Short silence

Bidding prayers

We bring our prayers to you, O God, from whom all families in heaven and on earth take their name.

We pray for all who have been gifted with the awesome responsibility of bearing, naming and raising children.
Call us all by name, O Lord, and hold us in your love.

We pray for all who bring their children to baptism or come to baptism themselves, that they may grow ever more deeply within the family of God.
Call us all by name, O Lord, and hold us in your love.

We pray for those who have no family or have lost touch with the family they once had.
Call us all by name, O Lord, and hold us in your love.

We pray for all who struggle to discover who they really are;
may they find their deepest identity in you.
Call us all by name, O Lord, and hold us in your love.

Collect

Gracious Father,
you called your Son Jesus
before he was conceived in Mary's womb,
and named him as our Saviour.
Help us to live in this world
as those who belong to your family.
Thank you that we are your children;
you have called us by name
and we are held securely in your loving embrace.
Amen

The Epiphany (6 January)

Opening prayer

*Open our eyes, O Lord, to the mystery of the water made wine,
that we may see the miracle of the divine love at work within the
everyday circumstances of our lives. Amen*

Reading

On the third day there was a wedding in Cana of Galilee,
and the mother of Jesus was there… When the wine gave
out, [she] said to him, 'They have no wine.' And Jesus said
to her, 'Woman, what concern is that to you and to me? My
hour has not yet come.' His mother said to the servants,
'Do whatever he tells you.' Now standing there were six
stone water-jars for the Jewish rites of purification, each
holding twenty or thirty gallons. Jesus said to them, 'Fill
the jars with water… Now draw some out, and take it to
the chief steward.'… When the steward tasted the water
that had become wine… [he] called the bridegroom and
said to him, 'Everyone serves the good wine first, and then
the inferior wine after the guests have become drunk. But
you have kept the good wine until now.' Jesus did this, the
first of his signs… and revealed his glory; and his disciples
believed in him.

JOHN 2:1–11 (ABRIDGED)

Reflection

At a wedding where the wine has run out, Jesus' mother—
ever practical and aware of her son's abilities—acts to avert
a potentially embarrassing situation for the bridegroom. 'Do

whatever he tells you,' she instructs the stewards. Jesus' response betrays real irritation—and why? 'My hour has not yet come.' His mother is pressurising him to declare himself before he feels the time is right.

Much scholarly ink has been spilled over the precise meaning of Jesus' 'hour'. What does seem clear is that it contains within it a sacred sense of *kairos*—God's time— precisely the right moment for something to be expressed or enacted. If Jesus were to act before this time, he knew that he would be viewed as a wonder-worker and nothing more; and, from his own desert experience, he knew only too well the subtle temptation to act the showman and cultivate an admiring audience.

So Jesus shields his hand. A miracle is performed, but most at the wedding are totally unaware of the fact. There is something of 'the wisdom of Solomon' (1 Kings 3:16–28) in Jesus' response. A practical crisis is averted, his mother is satisfied, the disciples are given a glimpse of his glory and they believe in him—but Jesus also safeguards his own position and, for most at this wedding, his power remains veiled.

Short silence

Bidding prayers

Our heavenly Father seeks to transform our lives through the touch of his love. Let us bring our prayers to him in confidence and trust.

In the love of Christ, may we seek to be channels of transformation amid the pain of this world.
Lord, help us to know the miracle of your transforming love.

In the love of Christ, may we seek to discern your time for our being and doing.
Lord, help us to know the miracle of your transforming love.

In the love of Christ, may we seek to reach out to all we meet with his compassion.
Lord, help us to know the miracle of your transforming love.

In the love of Christ, may we seek to become ever more grounded in the depths of our Father's love.
Lord, help us to know the miracle of your transforming love.

Collect

Heavenly Father,
at Cana your Son changed water into wine
and gave his disciples a glimpse of his glory.
Through the alchemy of your Spirit,
transform our sorrow into joy
and our mourning into dancing,
that our hearts may be invigorated
with the new wine of your kingdom.
We ask this in Jesus' name.
Amen

The Conversion of Paul
(25 January)

Opening prayer

Almighty God, you call us your children to transformation of life and growth in your love. Help us, we pray, to respond with courage, trusting you to redeem the past and equip us for a future beyond our imagining. We ask this in Jesus' name. Amen

Reading

'I was travelling to Damascus with the authority and commission of the chief priests, when at midday along the road, your Excellency, I saw a light from heaven, brighter than the sun... I heard a voice saying to me in the Hebrew language, 'Saul, Saul, why are you persecuting me? It hurts you to kick against the goads.' I asked, 'Who are you, Lord?' The Lord answered, 'I am Jesus whom you are persecuting. But get up and stand on your feet; for I have appeared to you for this purpose... I will rescue you from your people and from the Gentiles—to whom I am sending you to open their eyes so that they may turn from darkness to light.'

ACTS 26:12–18 (ABRIDGED)

Reflection

'Saul, Saul... It hurts you to kick against the goads' (v. 14). Paul's telling of his dramatic encounter with the risen Jesus resonates with the account in Acts 9, apart from this cryptic reference to 'goads'. A stick used for controlling cattle, a goad can also be defined as 'anything that torments, incites or stimulates' (*Oxford English Dictionary*). In context here, provocatively, it is clearly God who is doing the goading.

Throughout Christian history, some have held up Paul's experience as the only measure of true Christian conversion, and there are indeed people who find themselves brought to faith in this dramatic, even violent, fashion. But we limit the mysterious workings of God if we confine his transforming work in us to this method alone.

For every dramatic conversion, there are countless others whose journey into God is a silent, almost imperceptible growth into life in all its fullness. Many will be unable to pinpoint a defining moment, their experience telling rather of a slow, gradual deepening of relationship with a God who has always been present.

Paul's case was dramatic but our human nature inevitably means that we, too, 'kick against the goads'. In essence, our situation is no different: whatever our past, we are called by God to abandon our stubborn self-will and 'to learn to bear the beams of love'.[16]

Short silence

Bidding prayers

In humility and contrition we bring our prayers to God, who goads us into abundance of life in his kingdom.

In the Church of God, inspired and yet fragmented, we pray that the voice of God will be heard.
Shine in our darkness, and let there be light.

In the troubled places of our world, where people cry out for justice, we pray that the voice of God will be heard.
Shine in our darkness, and let there be light.

In the impoverished communities of our land, where people cry out for a just sharing of society's resources, we pray that the voice of God will be heard.
Shine in our darkness, and let there be light.

In the multifaceted complexity of our hearts, where we cry out for healing and forgiveness, we pray that the voice of God will be heard.
Shine in our darkness, and let there be light.

Collect

Lord God and heavenly Father,
you call us out of darkness into your own marvellous light.
Pierce through the shadows of our perversity and confusion
with the blinding shaft of your love,
that we may hear your word
and know the truth of ourselves
within the shining reality of your Son,
Jesus Christ our Lord.
Amen

The Presentation of Christ in the Temple (Candlemas) (2 February)

Opening prayer

Almighty God, we thank you that you offer yourself freely to those who wait in hope for your coming. We praise and thank you for the gift of your presence, and pray that we may be beacons of light in a world in need of your salvation. Amen

Reading

Now there was a man in Jerusalem whose name was Simeon; this man was righteous and devout, looking forward to the consolation of Israel, and the Holy Spirit rested on him... Guided by the Spirit, Simeon came into the temple; and when the parents brought in the child Jesus, to do for him what was customary under the law, Simeon took him in his arms... There was also a prophet, Anna the daughter of Phanuel, of the tribe of Asher. She was of a great age... At that moment she came, and began to praise God and to speak about the child to all who were looking for the redemption of Jerusalem.

LUKE 2:25–28, 36–38 (ABRIDGED)

Reflection

Simeon and Anna – for what, or whom, were these two elderly and devout people looking and waiting? How were they to know it when they saw it? How long were they to wait? The remarkable thing is that they did know, immediately and without doubt, that this small, helpless child was indeed the promised Messiah. Simeon's reaction—the canticle we know as the Nunc Dimittis—was his spontaneous reaction of gratitude and praise; Anna also praised God and began to speak about Jesus to all who would listen.

The call to wait is one of the hardest calls for us to accept. Humanly, we like to know where we are, what it is we are waiting for and how long the wait is likely to be. Yet this call to wait is one that we all share. We are called to live it day by day: to watch and wait longingly for the coming of our Lord, not just in the distant future or during the season of Advent, but in every moment of our lives. As Simeon and Anna were able to see the Messiah in the unlikely guise of a baby, so will we, in our patient watching, waiting and yearning, be enabled to detect the hidden Christ in the most unexpected of places.

Short silence

Bidding prayers

Let us bring our prayers to God, seeking his gifts of patience and persistence, and the willingness to see him in unlikely people and places.

For those whose waiting is without hope:
Make us channels of your peace, Lord, for our eyes have seen your salvation.

For those whose waiting is without anticipation or desire:
Make us channels of your peace, Lord, for our eyes have seen your salvation.

For those whose waiting is anxious or fearful:
Make us channels of your peace, Lord, for our eyes have seen your salvation.

For those whose waiting conceals a veiled seeking for God:
Make us channels of your peace, Lord, for our eyes have seen your salvation.

Collect

Creator God of time and eternity,
mysteriously enfleshed as a human babe,
in the darkness of our waiting, our longing and our yearning,
may we, with Simeon and Anna,
rejoice in the mysterious light of your infant life
and proclaim that our eyes have seen your salvation
birthed in our world,
for us and for all people.
Through Jesus Christ our Lord.
Amen

Joseph of Nazareth (19 March)

Opening prayer

Almighty God, we thank you for all those unsung lives through whom your kingdom has advanced and your love has been spread abroad in the world. In our discipleship, may we be content for our acts of love and service to be known only to you. Amen

Reading

[Jesus] came to his home town and began to teach the people in their synagogue, so that they were astounded and said, 'Where did this man get this wisdom and these deeds of power? Is not this the carpenter's son? Is not his mother called Mary? And are not his brothers James and Joseph and Simon and Judas? And are not all his sisters with us? Where then did this man get all this?'

MATTHEW 13:54–56

Reflection

Matthew and Luke present Joseph as an ordinary man caught up in extraordinary circumstances. Matthew's opening genealogy shows Joseph's descent from David, and Joseph's adoption of Jesus as his own son makes Jesus legally 'of David's line'. Matthew depicts him as a good man with a deep trust in God (1:18–25). The readings around Christmastime show how Jesus' birth and early survival depended on Joseph's obedience to God's direction, and, once settled in Nazareth, he created a quiet, ordinary life for his family.

Today's reading indicates how successfully Joseph achieved this. Jesus is teaching in the synagogue in his home town and his audience are amazed at his wisdom, but they are also bemused. Jesus comes from an ordinary family, no different from any other in the town, so where can he have got his extraordinary ability?

The ordinary life that was enabled by Joseph created the platform from which the adult Jesus was able to fulfil his destiny. Although Jesus may well have been aware that Joseph was not his biological father (Luke 2:49), the fact that he called his heavenly Father *Abba* ('Daddy': Mark 14:36) must surely reflect something of the security and love he experienced with Joseph in his early years. It is not always through the dramatically obvious that the will of God makes itself known; sometimes the kingdom advances through people like Joseph, living quiet lives of hidden trust and obedience.

Short silence

Bidding prayers

We bring our prayers in trust and confidence to God, who knows best the ways in which we can serve him.

When life feels boring and it seems that nothing ever happens, Creator God, your world cries out for love, forgiveness and healing. Help us to be bearers of your love among the people you have given us.
Content us, Lord, to serve you in the ordinary and the unspectacular.

When we feel envious of the lot of others:
Content us, Lord, to serve you in the ordinary and the unspectacular.

Help us to seek you in the people and circumstances you have given us:
Content us, Lord, to serve you in the ordinary and the unspectacular.

Help us to trust your placing of us within the wider growth of your kingdom.
Content us, Lord, to serve you in the ordinary and the unspectacular.

Collect

Heavenly Father,
through the faithful, quiet life of Joseph
you gave Jesus the love and security
of an earthly home.
We thank you, Lord,
for all those known to us and to you
who set our lives on firm foundations
and pointed us
to the reality and depth of your love.
In Jesus' name we pray.
Amen

The Annunciation (25 March)

Opening prayer

Dear Lord, as Mary consented to bear your Son, so you call us to bear the love of God in your world today. When we are fearful, calm our spirits and strengthen our resolve as we seek to respond to your call in faith and trust. Amen

Reading

In the sixth month the angel Gabriel was sent by God to a town in Galilee called Nazareth, to a virgin engaged to a man whose name was Joseph, of the house of David. The virgin's name was Mary. And he came to her and said, 'Greetings, favoured one! The Lord is with you.' But she was much perplexed by his words and pondered what sort of greeting this might be. The angel said to her, 'Do not be afraid, Mary, for you have found favour with God. And now, you will conceive in your womb and bear a son, and you will name him Jesus.'

LUKE 1:26–31

Reflection

We first met the 14th-century Sienese painter Simone Martini when reflecting on the twelve-year-old Jesus' visit to the temple in Jerusalem on the First Sunday of Christmas. In *The Story of Painting*, Sister Wendy Beckett draws our attention to another intriguing painting by Martini. Entitled *The Angel and the Annunciation*, it portrays the moment when the angel Gabriel, dazzling with golden colour, appears to

Mary and makes his disturbing request. And there is no doubt at all that Martini's Mary *is* disturbed. Her whole body shrinks away from the angel and she is quite clearly aghast at what is being asked of her. Yet she cannot quite tear her eyes away from the penetrating and compelling force of the angel's gaze.

It must have been a little like this, surely? However devout she was, however close her walk with God had been, up to this point in her life, Mary simply had no precedent to help her assess the angel's request. She was being asked to take a gigantic step into the unknown; the probable consequences were grave (Matthew 1:18–25) and potentially life-threatening.

'Doing the Lord's will' may not seem to be such a difficult thing when our circumstances are secure, our plans are made and we think we know where we are. But how do we react when unforeseen circumstances strike and God calls us to leave those securities behind?

Short silence

Bidding prayers

Let us come before our heavenly Father, who calms our fears, gives rest to our troubled souls and calls us to share his love in the world.

Creator God, your world cries out for love, forgiveness and healing. Help us to be bearers of your love in the places where we live and work.
Lord, I am your servant; let it be with me according to your word.

Creator God, your world cries out for love, forgiveness and healing. Help us to be bearers of your love among the people you have given us.

Lord, I am your servant; let it be with me according to your word.

Creator God, your world cries out for love, forgiveness and healing. Help us to reach out with compassion to those who suffer.

Lord, I am your servant; let it be with me according to your word.

Creator God, your world cries out for love, forgiveness and healing. Give us open ears and hearts, that, amid the clamour of the world's noise, we may hear and respond to your still, small voice.

Lord, I am your servant; let it be with me according to your word.

Collect

Heavenly Father,
you called Mary from the known securities of home and family
and invited her to be the mother of your Son.
Help us, like her, to respond to you
with courage and joy,
gladly placing our hand in yours
and trusting you for the unknown future.
In Jesus' name we pray.
Amen

Visit of the Blessed Virgin Mary to Elizabeth (31 May)

Opening prayer

Almighty God, we thank you that the beauty and splendour of your vibrant presence is all around us. Sharpen our spiritual senses, we pray, that we may perceive your glory in all those we meet and in all we see and do. We ask this in Jesus' name. Amen

Reading

In those days Mary set out and went with haste to a Judean town in the hill country, where she entered the house of Zechariah and greeted Elizabeth. When Elizabeth heard Mary's greeting, the child leapt in her womb. And Elizabeth was filled with the Holy Spirit and exclaimed with a loud cry, 'Blessed are you among women, and blessed is the fruit of your womb… And blessed is she who believed that there would be a fulfilment of what was spoken to her by the Lord.'

LUKE 1:39–42, 45

Reflection

Frequently in the Gospel narrative, ordinary experiences of daily life transmute into something extraordinary. Water is turned into wine to save the embarrassment of the host at a wedding feast (John 2:1–11); a hungry multitude are fed and satisfied (Luke 9:12–17); a routine fishing expedition seems to end in failure and, then, miraculously, produces a super-abundant catch of fish (John 21:4–8).

So it is with today's narrative. Mary knows she is pregnant

and has been told by the angel that her older relative Elizabeth is also expecting a child. Mary's response is understandable and natural: she sets out 'with haste' to visit Elizabeth, so that they may rejoice together and offer support to one another in a very precious shared human experience.

But the moment of meeting between the two women shifts a natural experience into the supernatural dimension. Without apparently being told, Elizabeth immediately recognises Mary as the mother of her Lord (v. 43), and, as the baby in Elizabeth's womb leaps in like recognition, the bond between Jesus and the Baptist is forged.

The phrase 'heaven in ordinarie', coined by the 16th-century priest-poet George Herbert, captures brilliantly the experience of transcendence that can catch us unawares in the midst of our ordinary daily routine. The teaching of scripture and of the spiritual wisdom of the ages is that such glimpses of glory are all around us, if only we have eyes to see.

Short silence

Bidding prayers

We offer our prayers to our heavenly Father, seeking a renewal of our lives in the power and gentleness of his Spirit.

Holy God, widen our vision.
Spirit of God, fill us, that we may discern the glory of God in all things.

Holy God, sharpen our insight.
Spirit of God, fill us, that we may discern the glory of God in all things.

Holy God, increase our love.
Spirit of God, fill us, that we may discern the glory of God in all things.

Holy God, deepen our gratitude.
Spirit of God, fill us, that we may discern the glory of God in all things.

Collect

God of wonder and delight,
your mercies are new every morning.
Quicken us with your Spirit, we pray,
that with vision cleansed
and hearts renewed,
we may perceive and rejoice in the glory
concealed within the things of this world.
We ask this in Jesus' name.
Amen

Birth of John the Baptist (24 June)

Opening prayer

Almighty God, stir us, we pray, that we may share in the work of proclaiming the coming of your kingdom on earth. In Jesus' name we pray. Amen

Reading

Now the time came for Elizabeth to give birth, and she bore a son...On the eighth day they came to circumcise the child, and they were going to name him Zechariah after his father. But his mother said, 'No; he is to be called John,' ... Then his father Zechariah was filled with the Holy Spirit and spoke this prophecy: 'Blessed be the Lord God of Israel, for he has looked favourably on his people and redeemed them... Thus he has shown the mercy promised to our ancestors, and has remembered his holy covenant, the oath that he swore to our ancestor Abraham... And you, child, will be called the prophet of the Most High; for you will go before the Lord to prepare his ways, to give knowledge of salvation to his people by the forgiveness of their sins. By the tender mercy of our God, the dawn from on high will break upon us, to give light to those who sit in darkness and in the shadow of death, to guide our feet into the way of peace.' The child grew and became strong in spirit, and he was in the wilderness until the day he appeared publicly to Israel.

LUKE 1:57–60, 67–68, 72–73, 76–80 (ABRIDGED)

Reflection

Zechariah's prayer of thanksgiving and blessing on the birth of his son John the Baptist is familiar to us as the liturgical canticle Benedictus. John's birth was preceded by a considerable degree of mystery and personal trauma for his parents: not only were both Zechariah and Elizabeth old, making her childbearing highly unlikely, but, because of Zechariah's doubts, the angel declared that he would be dumb for the duration of his wife's pregnancy (Luke 1:18–20).

The child, the herald of Christ's coming, is born; Zechariah's tongue is released and, in the power of the Spirit, his words pour forth in a paean of praise and thanksgiving. But there is so much more to this than the prayer of a relieved and grateful father. Zechariah's words look back to God's early covenantal promise to Abraham, and to the Israelites' centuries-long night of waiting, praying and longing for the coming of God's promised Messiah.

Through these words, Luke is also reminding his readers that the births of both John the Baptist and Jesus came at a time when Israel was struggling under the political domination of Rome and of Herod, its vassal-king. With the births of these two children, God's promise of hope and redemption is spoken to the people in the very heart of their oppression and suffering.

Short silence

Bidding prayers

As God calls us to serve and point the way to Christ, let us bring our prayers in confidence and trust to our heavenly Father.

Help us to respond to your call to serve.
Blessed Lord, you guide our feet into the way of peace.

Help us to comfort those who sit in darkness.
Blessed Lord, you guide our feet into the way of peace.

Help us to point to Christ, the Light of the world.
Blessed Lord, you guide our feet into the way of peace.

Help us to play our part in preparing the way of the Lord.
Blessed Lord, you guide our feet into the way of peace.

Collect

Almighty Father,
in your wisdom
you called your servant John the Baptist
to prepare the way for your Son.
Sharpen our ears to your voice,
consecrating us as heralds of your gospel,
and deepen our willingness
to live as harbingers of your kingdom of peace and love.
In Jesus' name we pray.
Amen

Peter the Apostle (29 June)

Opening prayer

Heavenly Father, help us this day to come to you with our sin and our weakness. May we know that our fragility is no barrier to you, if we will only trust in your power to heal and forgive. In Jesus' name we pray. Amen

Reading

When they had finished breakfast, Jesus said to Simon Peter, 'Simon son of John, do you love me more than these? He said to him, 'Yes, Lord; you know that I love you.' Jesus said to him, 'Feed my lambs.' A second time he said to him, 'Simon son of John, do you love me?' He said to him, 'Yes, Lord; you know that I love you.' Jesus said to him, 'Tend my sheep.' He said to him the third time, 'Simon son of John, do you love me?' Peter felt hurt because he said to him the third time, 'Do you love me?' And he said to him, 'Lord, you know everything; you know that I love you.' Jesus said to him, 'Feed my sheep.'

JOHN 21:15–17

Reflection

Jesus' persistent, threefold questioning must have been agony for Peter. It seemed to him that Jesus needed to be convinced of his love, and the memories of Peter's threefold denial of Jesus on the night of his arrest must have been sharply present between them. In the words of Tom Wright, 'the smell of the charcoal fire lingers',[17] and Peter must not have known what to do with himself.

And Jesus' reaction? 'Feed my sheep.' No recriminations; no anger; no 'get yourself sorted out and then I might be able to trust you again'. His reaction, amazingly, is to entrust Peter with the care of his flock, to give him the responsibility of leading the post-resurrection, post-ascension Church.

What an encouragement and reassurance there is in this for us! Peter's cowardice, desperate and painful though it was, was ultimately no impediment to Jesus. We know, all too well, our tendency to trip and fall. Intellectually, we also know that 'we have this treasure in clay jars, so that it may be made clear that this extraordinary power belongs to God and does not come from us' (2 Corinthians 4:7), but we struggle to believe it emotionally. Can Jesus really use someone as weak and fallible as I am? If we will hear it, Peter's experience here gives the answer.

Short silence

Bidding prayers

We bring our prayers to our heavenly Father, who knows both our weakness and our love.

When we let others down and leave them to face their difficulties alone,
Heal and forgive us, Lord, and use us in the work of your kingdom.

When we feel paralysed and unable to forgive ourselves for the wrong we have done,
Heal and forgive us, Lord, and use us in the work of your kingdom.

When we find ourselves paralysed and unable to forgive the wrongs done to us,
Heal and forgive us, Lord, and use us in the work of your kingdom.

When you call us, despite ourselves, to share in the fullness of your love,
Heal and forgive us, Lord, and use us in the work of your kingdom.

Collect

Loving heavenly Father,
despite failure and denial
you restored Peter to loving fellowship
and renewed his call to serve you.
Forgive us when we fail, and heal our wounds,
strengthen our love
and renew us in the work and ministry
to which you have called us
in Jesus Christ our Lord.
Amen

Thomas the Apostle (3 July)

Opening prayer

Heavenly Father, we pray this day for the courage and grace to look to you alone for our security and reassurance. We ask this in Jesus' name. Amen

Reading

But Thomas (who was called the Twin), one of the twelve, was not with them when Jesus came. So the other disciples told him, 'We have seen the Lord.' But he said to them, 'Unless I see the mark of the nails in his hands, and put my finger in the mark of the nails and my hand in his side, I will not believe.' A week later his disciples were again in the house, and Thomas was with them. Although the doors were shut, Jesus came and stood among them and said, 'Peace be with you.' Then he said to Thomas, 'Put your finger here and see my hands. Reach out your hand and put it in my side. Do not doubt but believe.' Thomas answered him, 'My Lord and my God!' Jesus said to him, 'Have you believed because you have seen? Blessed are those who have not seen, and yet have come to believe.'

JOHN 20:24–29

Reflection

Poor old Thomas has gone down in the annals of history as the disciple who doubted; indeed, the phrase 'doubting Thomas' has become a byword for one who refuses to believe. But is this fair? Was Thomas the only one to doubt?

In various ways, all the disciples doubted. Judas betrayed Jesus; Peter denied him; when Jesus was crucified they all deserted him; when the women told them that Jesus had risen, they did not believe it (Luke 24:11).

No, Thomas was not the only doubter, and the Benedictine monk Thomas Keating offers an intriguingly different interpretation of this incident. Thomas was absent when Jesus first appeared to the disciples (John 20:19–23) and Keating suggests that Thomas' 'disbelief' was a psychological reaction stemming from feelings of hurt and rejection rather than a lack of faith. What was wrong with him? Why had Jesus appeared to the others and not to him?

Perhaps the model that Thomas provides for us is slightly different than we thought. It is not that some have doubts and others do not. Doubt is a natural component of all faith; if not, faith is merely an attempt to grasp an illusory certainty. But we are all prone, at times, to the kind of insecurity Thomas displayed: the ego-need to feel acceptance and approval; the temptation to look for human security and reassurance rather than rely on God alone.

Short silence

Bidding prayers

We have a God who knows us in all our weakness and human need. We bring our prayers to him in confidence and trust.

We see in a mirror, dimly: we pray for our troubled world.
Blessed are those who have not seen, and yet have come to believe.

We see in a mirror, dimly: we pray for the poverty and suffering in society.
Blessed are those who have not seen, and yet have come to believe.

We see in a mirror, dimly: we pray for ourselves and our tendency to seek security in 'signs' rather than in God alone.
Blessed are those who have not seen, and yet have come to believe.

We see in a mirror, dimly: we pray with longing for the time when we shall see you face to face.
Blessed are those who have not seen, and yet have come to believe.

Collect

Almighty God,
you met Thomas in his human frailty
and graced him
with the signs of your risen life.
Strengthen us, we pray,
in our weakness and insecurity,
and lead us to place our trust and confidence
in you alone.
We ask this in Jesus' name.
Amen

Mary Magdalene (22 July)

Opening prayer

Heavenly Father, give us the eyes of faith to see the presence of your Son in all our encounters today. We ask this in Jesus' name. Amen

Reading

Mary stood weeping outside the tomb. As she wept, she bent over to look into the tomb; and she saw two angels in white, sitting where the body of Jesus had been lying... They said to her, 'Woman, why are you weeping?' She said to them, 'They have taken away my Lord, and I do not know where they have laid him.' When she had said this, she turned round and saw Jesus standing there, but she did not know it was Jesus... Supposing him to be the gardener, she said to him, 'Sir, if you have carried him away, tell me where you have laid him, and I will take him away.' Jesus said to her, 'Mary!' She turned and said to him in Hebrew, 'Rabbouni!' (which means Teacher).

JOHN 20:11–16 (ABRIDGED)

Reflection

It is not easy for us to put ourselves into the shoes of Jesus' closest followers in the devastating hours following his crucifixion. All the Gospels name Mary Magdalene as one of the women closest to Jesus, and she is described as having been healed by Jesus before accompanying him in his ministry. It is hard for us to imagine the depths of her sorrow and devastation as she comes to the tomb alone in the pre-dawn darkness and finds it empty. Blinded by her grief, she seeks the help of one whom she takes to be the gardener.

But Jesus calls her by her name, and in the intimacy of that calling comes amazed and incredulous recognition. She impulsively reaches out to the one she loves and thought she had lost, but Jesus has a vital task for her: 'Go to my brothers and say to them, "I am ascending to my Father and your Father, to my God and your God"' (v. 17).

When we are in despair, it is hard to believe that we shall ever again know a renewal of life and love. But even in such dark times, God reaches out to us as he did to Mary Magdalene, calling us by name and charging us with his message of hope to a needy world.

Short silence

Bidding prayers

Let us pray with confidence to God, who reaches out to us in our distress.

When life is dark and future hopes and dreams seem brutally quenched:
Within the darkness, may we hear you call our name.

When life is dark and we can see no way out of our pain:
Within the darkness, may we hear you call our name.

When life is dark and we misunderstand the loving presence of those closest to us:
Within the darkness, may we hear you call our name.

When life is dark and we need your divine presence to ignite us with hope for the future:
Within the darkness, may we hear you call our name.

Collect

Loving God,
you appeared to Mary Magdalene in her sorrow and distress
and spoke to her of new life and hope.
Breathe into the darkness of our despair
the reality of your presence,
and strengthen our calling
to witness to the world the wonder of your risen love.
We ask this in Jesus' name.
Amen

Mary, Martha and Lazarus
(29 July)

Opening prayer

Heavenly Father, we pray that you would give us the grace to live this day with hospitable hearts. May we be open to friend and stranger, striving to see in all the face of Christ. In Jesus' name we pray. Amen

Reading

Six days before the Passover Jesus came to Bethany, the home of Lazarus, whom he had raised from the dead. There they gave a dinner for him. Martha served, and Lazarus was one of those at the table with him. Mary took a pound of costly perfume made of pure nard, anointed Jesus' feet, and wiped them with her hair. The house was filled with the fragrance of the perfume.

JOHN 12:1–3

Reflection

We have spent some time with these verses before, as part of our reflection for Monday of Holy Week, but the focus here is very different. We are concerned not with the precise details of what is going on in this passage but with the snapshot it gives of the hospitality offered to Jesus by Mary, Martha and Lazarus.

We never hear Lazarus' voice, although his raising to life by Jesus is the focus of one of the most critical episodes in the Gospels (John 11). Here, Lazarus is the host of a dinner given in Jesus' honour, possibly in gratitude for his recent restoration to life. Mary and Martha are more familiar to us, and each is presented in her accustomed role: Martha is serving at table and Mary, in her anointing of Jesus' feet, takes her contemplative listening to Jesus to a new level.

For Jesus, in an extraordinary life marked by increasing tension, misunderstanding and outright conflict, the steady, constant friendship of the household at Bethany must have been like an oasis in the desert. Most of us will not be called upon to live out our lives and Christian calling in the public arena that Jesus endured, but the opportunities we are given to offer hospitality to others along the way may enable the furtherance of God's will and purpose in the world in ways we cannot even begin to imagine.

Short silence

Bidding prayers

In hope and trust we come before God, whose hospitable heart is always open to our prayers and cries of need.

In the troubled places of our world, where it is sometimes difficult to recognise the presence of Christ,
May we welcome you, Lord, in the friend and the stranger.

In the experiences of conflict and misunderstanding in our church communities, where it is sometimes difficult to recognise the presence of Christ,
May we welcome you, Lord, in the friend and the stranger.

In those dark and hidden places of our own hearts, where it is sometimes difficult to recognise the presence of Christ,
May we welcome you, Lord, in the friend and the stranger.

In those experiences of joyous welcome and celebration,
when we recognise Christ in the person before us,
May we welcome you, Lord, in the friend and the stranger.

Collect

Lord Jesus Christ,
in the home of Mary, Martha and Lazarus
you found friendship, love, and respite
from the noise and judgment of the world.
Give us hospitable hearts, we pray,
content to serve you in the homely and unspectacular;
and may others find a home in us
where they find welcome and acceptance.
For your name's sake we pray.
Amen

The Transfiguration of our Lord (6 August)

Opening prayer

Almighty God, we pray that in our daily lives you would grant us glimpses of your glory, that we may know the world to be shot through with the grandeur and radiance of your presence. We ask this in Jesus' name. Amen

Reading

Six days later, Jesus took with him Peter and James and John, and led them up a high mountain apart, by themselves. And he was transfigured before them, and his clothes became dazzling white, such as no one on earth could bleach them. And there appeared to them Elijah with Moses, who were talking with Jesus. Then Peter said to Jesus, 'Rabbi, it is good for us to be here; let us make three dwellings, one for you, one for Moses, and one for Elijah.' He did not know what to say, for they were terrified. Then a cloud overshadowed them, and from the cloud there came a voice, 'This is my Son, the Beloved; listen to him!' Suddenly when they looked round, they saw no one with them any more, but only Jesus.

MARK 9:2–8

Reflection

'This is my Son, the Beloved...' Once before, at Jesus' baptism, a voice from a cloud declared these words (Matthew 3:17; Luke 3:22; Mark 1:11). Both then and on the present occasion, the veil obscuring Christ's divinity was momentarily lifted, giving a glimpse of the glory beyond. Taking Peter, James and John with him, Jesus has gone up the mountain to pray, but this scene, familiar as it must have been to the disciples, is to turn into something awesome and mysterious.

In a powerful meditation on a 15th-century icon of the transfiguration, Rowan Williams comments on the extra-ordinary energy of the scene: 'Christ, his robes pure white, stands on a rocky outcrop… against a background of darker colour, red or deep blue or both… Moses and Elijah stand on peaks of rock one on each side, and further down the very steep and craggy mountain are the disciples, sprawled in disorder.'[18] Through a process of divine alchemy, the base metal of the routine and everyday is transformed into the pure gold of divine encounter, and Williams goes on to describe how the Gospel account and the rich symbolism of the icon show us the radiance beyond the veil. Christ is our portal into the inexhaustible mystery and riches of God, and, in him, all our experience is capable of renewal and transformation.

Short silence

Bidding prayers

In faith, trust and awe we bring our prayers to God, who transfigures our lives and experience through the radiance of his glory.

In the patterns and rhythms of the daily round:
Transfigure us, we pray, with the glory of your presence.

In the fears and anxieties that so often paralyse us:
Transfigure us, we pray, with the glory of your presence.

In our work and our relationships:
Transfigure us, we pray, with the glory of your presence.

In our prayer and our seeking to ground our lives in the reality of your beloved Son:
Transfigure us, we pray, with the glory of your presence.

Collect

Almighty God,
in Christ transfigured on the mountain, you showed the disciples
the continuity of all that is and has been
in the unity of your loving purpose.
In the complexity of our lives, grant us visions of your radiance,
that we may hear your voice
and glimpse the glory within the cloud.
We ask this in Jesus' name.
Amen

The Blessed Virgin Mary
(15 August)

Opening prayer

*Heavenly Father, we pray that you would hold and keep us this day,
so that, following the example of Mary, we may live our lives with
open, trusting and generous hearts. We ask this in Jesus' name.
Amen*

Reading

And Mary said, 'My soul magnifies the Lord, and my spirit
rejoices in God my Saviour, for he has looked with favour
on the lowliness of his servant. Surely, from now on all
generations will call me blessed; for the Mighty One has
done great things for me, and holy is his name. His mercy
is for those who fear him from generation to generation.
He has shown strength with his arm; he has scattered the
proud in the thoughts of their hearts... he has filled the
hungry with good things, and sent the rich away empty.
He has helped his servant Israel, in remembrance of his
mercy, according to the promise he made to our ancestors,
to Abraham and to his descendants for ever.'

LUKE 1:46–55 (ABRIDGED)

Reflection

Today is kept as the major feast celebrating the Virgin Mary
throughout Christendom, both East and West. Although
some of the most ancient manuscripts put this passage into
the mouth of Elizabeth, the paean of praise that we know

today as the Magnificat has, during centuries of church tradition, been attributed to Mary.

As we have journeyed through the church's year, we have seen glimpses of Mary, usually at critical times in the life of her son—puzzling at the wonder and mystery surrounding Christ's birth; worrying over her twelve-year-old son, lost in Jerusalem; nudging him towards reluctant action when the wine runs out at a wedding feast. She experienced the unimaginable agony of seeing her son die on a cross and, after his resurrection, was present in Jerusalem as a member of the early Christian community.

We see in her the joys and anxieties of motherhood and the tensions in family relationships, her struggles to understand the 'difference' of her son, and her agony and sense of helplessness as she witnesses his suffering. But her faith sustains her and, after Christ's ascension, she is part of the praying group of disciples in Jerusalem (Acts 1:14). As the mother of Christ, Mary's situation is unique, but it nevertheless offers us a pattern of response within a deepening relationship to God, which is relevant to our own lives.

Short silence

Bidding prayers

In humility and thankfulness we bring our prayers to God, before whom every knee shall bow.

We pray for the leaders of the world, that they may govern with wisdom and justice.
My soul magnifies the Lord, and my spirit rejoices in God my Saviour.

We pray for those given the responsibility of great wealth, that they may live with thankful and generous hearts.
My soul magnifies the Lord, and my spirit rejoices in God my Saviour.

We pray that all hearts would be touched, and that we may work together for a just and more equal sharing of the earth's resources.
My soul magnifies the Lord, and my spirit rejoices in God my Saviour.

We pray for a humbling of excessive pride and ambition, and that we may be able to distinguish need from greed.
My soul magnifies the Lord, and my spirit rejoices in God my Saviour.

Collect

Heavenly Father,
you called Mary within the obscurity of a hidden life
to be the mother of your Son.
In a world of ego-driven ambition and instant celebrity,
may we be content to be known by you alone.
Help us to respond to your call in our own time and place
to be God-bearers of your Son,
and to be content to serve you in the shadows
with courage, obedience and joy.
We ask this in Jesus' name.
Amen

Bartholomew (24 August)

Opening prayer

Almighty God, we pray that you would help us resist the tempta-
tion to approach life with a jaded and world-weary cynicism,
enabling us instead to live and work today in the glorious light of
your kingdom. We ask this in Jesus' name. Amen

Reading

The next day Jesus decided to go to Galilee. He found Philip
and said to him, 'Follow me.' ... Philip found Nathanael
and said to him, 'We have found him about whom Moses
in the law and also the prophets wrote, Jesus son of Joseph
from Nazareth.' Nathanael said to him, 'Can anything good
come out of Nazareth?' Philip said to him, 'Come and see.'
When Jesus saw Nathanael coming toward him, he said of
him, 'Here is truly an Israelite in whom there is no deceit!'
Nathanael asked him, 'Where did you come to know me?'
Jesus answered, 'I saw you under the fig tree before Philip
called you.' Nathanael replied, 'Rabbi, you are the Son of
God! You are the King of Israel!' Jesus answered, 'Do you
believe because I told you that I saw you under the fig tree?
You will see greater things than these.' And he said to him,
'Very truly, I tell you, you will see heaven opened and the
angels of God ascending and descending upon the Son of
Man.'

JOHN 1:43–51

Reflection

Church tradition has long assumed that Bartholomew and Nathanael are the same person, although we cannot be absolutely certain. Nathanael is not named as a disciple in any of the Gospel lists (Matthew 10:2–4; Mark 3:16–18; Luke 6:14–16), but Bartholomew is there, placed alongside Philip each time. It is in John that the disciple's name is given as Nathanael, and it may be that the association with Philip, as in today's passage, is in part what has led to the conflation of the two.

In addition to the confusion of names, there are other puzzling features to the call of Nathanael, and the event recorded here does not yield itself to straightforward interpretation. Philip tells Nathanael about Jesus, and Nathanael's cynical response (v. 46) is the first time that witness to Jesus has met with any kind of resistance. He does, however, accept Philip's invitation to 'Come and see', and begins to experience Jesus as someone who knows him from the inside (vv. 47–48).

Nathanael's transition from scepticism to capitulation (v. 49) is surprisingly abrupt, as Jesus' comment also makes clear (v. 50), but we shouldn't worry too much about this. The point of the story is the profound effect on Nathanael of Jesus' supernatural insight into his character. Nathanael recognised Jesus' knowledge of him, as a revelation, and it drew him from a world-weary cynicism to faith in Jesus as the Son of God.

Short silence

Bidding prayers

Our heavenly Father understands our weariness and lack of confidence; we bring our prayers to him in hope and trust.

When the weight of the world lies heavy on our shoulders:
You invite us, Lord, to 'Come and see.'

When we are weary, and fear that we have no strength to respond to your call:
You invite us, Lord, to 'Come and see.'

When it seems to us that the cynics of this world have the upper hand:
You invite us, Lord, to 'Come and see.'

When we lose confidence in your ability to help and strengthen us:
You invite us, Lord, to 'Come and see.'

Collect

Lord Jesus Christ,
you call us from behind our self-imposed barriers
of fear and cynicism
and invite us to 'Come and see.'
Enable us, like Nathanael,
to take a leap of faith,
that we may come to know ourselves
as you know us,
as children beloved of the Father.
We ask this in your name.
Amen

The Beheading of John the Baptist (29 August)

Opening prayer

Heavenly Father, we pray that you would help us this day not to be over-reliant on the approval of others or the visible results of our work, but to trust rather in your patient outworking of all things to your glory. In Jesus' name we pray. Amen

Reading

But when Herod's birthday came, the daughter of Herodias danced before the company, and she pleased Herod so much that he promised on oath to grant her whatever she might ask. Prompted by her mother, she said, 'Give me the head of John the Baptist here on a platter.' The king was grieved, yet out of regard for his oaths and for the guests, he commanded it to be given; he sent and had John beheaded in the prison. The head was brought on a platter and given to the girl, who brought it to her mother. His disciples came and took the body and buried it; then they went and told Jesus.

MATTHEW 14:6–12

Reflection

After John was thrown into prison for daring to criticise the morality of the king's brother and sister-in-law, his life, like that of many prophets before him, was on a knife edge. Matthew indicates that it was only fear of public opinion that had so far prevented Herod from killing John (v. 5), and, at his birthday party, it was again fear of public opinion that led him to order John's beheading (v. 9). John was given no glimmer of light or reassurance at the end: to all appearances, his life's work ended in abject failure. The last we see of him is when his disciples take his headless corpse away for burial.

And yet… we are invited to take a wider view, one that John and his disciples could not possibly have guessed at. For post-Ascension believers, John's experience prefigures the death of Jesus, whose life also appeared to end in total defeat. Jesus' body, too, was taken away for burial, but on the third day God raised him from the dead.

When we are under threat, and our cherished enterprises—even the God-given ones—collapse before our eyes, it is within this wider perspective that we too need to take heart. A call to serve is no guarantee of worldly success and approval, but in Christ we are challenged to raise our hearts in trust and hope to the completion of all things in him.

Short silence

Bidding prayers

In hope and trust, we bring our prayers to the Lord of all time and eternity.

When the state of the world depresses us and we have no hope of any real change:
Kindle our hope, Lord, in the promise of your resurrection.

When we know only too well the entanglement of good and evil in our own hearts:
Kindle our hope, Lord, in the promise of your resurrection.

When we know ourselves to be a part of a greedy and acquisitive society, but aspire to live differently:
Kindle our hope, Lord, in the promise of your resurrection.

When we are depressed and downhearted and see no visible 'success' in our work for you:
Kindle our hope, Lord, in the promise of your resurrection.

Collect

Almighty God,
your servant John the Baptist
endured a painful and humiliating death
at the hands of an unjust and ungodly ruler.
When we are misjudged and treated with contempt,
and even our work for you seems doomed to fail,
give us hope, we pray,
in the promise of resurrection
and the taking up of all things
into the fullness of your glorious kingdom.
We ask this in Jesus' name.
Amen

Matthew, Apostle and Evangelist (21 September)

Opening prayer

Heavenly Father, you call us as individuals to love and serve you in the world. Help us, we pray, to see others as you see them, for you judge the heart and not the outward appearance. We ask this in Jesus' name. Amen

Reading

As Jesus was walking along, he saw a man called Matthew sitting at the tax booth; and he said to him, 'Follow me.' And he got up and followed him. And as he sat at dinner in the house, many tax collectors and sinners came and were sitting with him and his disciples. When the Pharisees saw this, they said to his disciples, 'Why does your teacher eat with tax collectors and sinners?' But when he heard this, he said, 'Those who are well have no need of a physician, but those who are sick. Go and learn what this means, "I desire mercy, not sacrifice." For I have come to call not the righteous but sinners.'

MATTHEW 9:9–13

Reflection

This passage is a parallel to the one in Luke 5:29–32, which we considered at Trinity 3 (see page 148). There, and in Mark's version of the incident (2:13–17), the tax collector is named Levi but the various names have generally been assumed to refer to the same person. Whatever the name, the message conveyed here is a powerful one. As a despised tax collector, Matthew was considered beyond the pale, and Jesus scandalised the authorities by associating with him. But Jesus' actions powerfully reinforce the teaching that God judges not the outward appearance but the heart.

We remember Matthew today and we also reflect on the first-century Gospel that bears his name. From the tone of the writing, it seems that Matthew's church community was composed of mainly Jewish (rather than Gentile) Christians, and they clearly knew their scriptures very well indeed (Matthew makes more than 130 references to the Hebrew scriptures). The French scholar Etienne Charpentier highlights a powerful experience of 'double vision' when reading the Gospel, stating that, with Matthew, we are never quite sure whether we are present at the time of Jesus or whether we are celebrating with the post-resurrection liturgy of the early Church. 'Thus the countenance of Jesus of Nazareth is revealed to us through the glorious features of the risen Lord celebrated by the church.'[19]

Short silence

Bidding prayers

We bring our prayers to our heavenly Father, who knows our ugliness and loveliness, our weaknesses and our strengths.

Help us, we pray, to see your light shining in the dark places of our world.
Lord, you have come to call not the righteous, but sinners.

Help us, we pray, to see your love at work in unexpected people and places.
Lord, you have come to call not the righteous, but sinners.

Help us, we pray, to see your face in the hostile and the unlovely.
Lord, you have come to call not the righteous, but sinners.

Help us, we pray, to know your presence in the shadows.
Lord, you have come to call not the righteous, but sinners.

Collect

Almighty God,
you called Matthew, the collector of taxes,
to be a follower of your Son.
May we, like him,
be prepared to leave all and follow you;
may we, like Jesus,
be prepared to see hope, promise and potential
in those whom the world despises.
In Jesus' name we pray.
Amen

Luke the Evangelist (18 October)

Opening prayer

Heavenly Father, as we go about our work this day, we pray that you would gift us with minds and spirits that are open to the world, and hearts that overflow with the love of Christ for all creation. In Jesus' name we pray. Amen

Reading

Since many have undertaken to set down an orderly account of the events that have been fulfilled among us, just as they were handed on to us by those who from the beginning were eyewitnesses and servants of the word, I too decided, after investigating everything carefully from the very first, to write an orderly account for you, most excellent Theophilus, so that you may know the truth concerning the things about which you have been instructed.

LUKE 1:1–4

Reflection

Luke was not one of the original group of disciples but was a dear friend of the apostle Paul. Paul mentions Luke three times in his letters, where he is described as a fellow worker (Philemon 24), as 'the beloved physician' (Colossians 4:14), and as Paul's only companion in prison (2 Timothy 4:11). He is believed to be the author of both the Gospel bearing his name and its sequel, the Acts of the Apostles. The link between the two is strong, as Acts 1:1 also names Theophilus as the addressee and refers back to the earlier work.

These first few verses of Luke's Gospel provide the frame-work for the narrative that is about to unfold. Three words are key to events that will recur in the Gospel: 'fulfilled' (v. 1, referring to God's redemptive acts in the past history of Israel); 'eyewitnesses' (v. 2, stressing the importance of the witness of those who had been with Jesus); and 'truth' (v. 4, of which the reader can be assured because of the experience of God's faithfulness in the past).

As a Gentile, Luke conveys powerfully in his writing that the good news of Christ is for all, regardless of gender, social position or nationality. Of all the Gospel writers, Luke perhaps comes across as the warmest, with heart and spirit open to the world, seeking to embrace all within the love of Christ.

Short silence

Bidding prayers

In faith and trust we bring our prayers to our heavenly Father, whose heart of love embraces the whole of creation.

Visit us with your mercy and forgiveness, O God, in a world where many experience injustice and persecution.
For the dawn from on high will break upon us.

Visit us with your mercy and forgiveness, O God, in a church where some experience exclusion and discrimination.
For the dawn from on high will break upon us.

Visit us with your mercy and forgiveness, O God; enlarge our hearts and widen our vision.
For the dawn from on high will break upon us.

Visit us with your mercy and forgiveness, O God; may our lives radiate the joy that knows your all-embracing love.
For the dawn from on high will break upon us.

Collect

Almighty God,
whose self-forgetful love flows out
to embrace the length and breadth,
the height and depth of all creation,
give us, with Luke,
a warm and pastoral heart,
a heart that refuses to judge and exclude
but rejoices to see friend and stranger alike
enfolded within the security
of Christ's loving embrace.
We ask this in Jesus' name.
Amen

Andrew the Apostle
(30 November)

Opening prayer

Almighty God, we thank you that you call us to serve you. Teach us humility, we pray, and a glad acceptance of the places where you put us and the tasks you call us to fulfil. In Jesus' name we pray. Amen

Reading

The next day John again was standing with two of his disciples, and as he watched Jesus walk by, he exclaimed, 'Look, here is the Lamb of God!' The two disciples heard him say this, and they followed Jesus. When Jesus turned and saw them following, he said to them, 'What are you looking for?' They said to him, 'Rabbi... where are you staying?' He said to them, 'Come and see.' ... One of the two who heard John speak and followed him was Andrew, Simon Peter's brother. He first found his brother Simon and said to him, 'We have found the Messiah.' ... He brought Simon to Jesus, who looked at him and said, 'You are Simon son of John. You are to be called Cephas' (which is translated Peter).

JOHN 1:35–42 (ABRIDGED)

Reflection

Today we reflect on the fourth Gospel's version of the call of the early disciples, including that of Andrew and his brother

Simon Peter. This account differs from those found in the Synoptic Gospels: rather than being called from his nets by Jesus, along with his brother, Andrew is presented here as a disciple of John the Baptist. John identifies Jesus as the Lamb of God (v. 36), and Andrew promptly switches his allegiance to Jesus, to whom he then introduces his brother Simon.

We may imagine that this must have been difficult for John, as he began to lose disciples to Jesus. Yet he appears to have lived out consistently his teaching in regard to Jesus: 'He must increase, but I must decrease' (John 3:30). Andrew must have learned well from his first teacher. Having introduced his brother to Jesus, the Gospels do not record any unhappiness on his part as he saw Peter become, with James and John, part of Jesus' inner circle of disciples and eventually the leader of them all.

Humanly, we tend to think in terms of hierarchy and the 'pecking order', and our egos bruise easily when we think we have been overlooked. But the humility of Andrew and his willingness to accept the precedence given to his brother challenge us with a radically different perspective.

Short silence

Bidding prayers

The secrets of all hearts are open to God; in humility and trust we bring our prayers to him.

Forgive our pride, Lord, and the times when we exaggerate our own importance in the scheme of things.
For our ways are not your ways, neither are our thoughts your thoughts.

Forgive our envy, Lord, when we see others given privileges that we believe are our due.
For our ways are not your ways, neither are our thoughts your thoughts.

Forgive our resentment, Lord, when we imagine that others are being advanced ahead of us on the way.
For our ways are not your ways, neither are our thoughts your thoughts.

Forgive our pettiness, Lord, when we lose sight of the vision of your all-embracing love.
For our ways are not your ways, neither are our thoughts your thoughts.

Collect

Heavenly Father,
you call us to your service
and use us in ways that challenge
our self-centredness
and sense of entitlement.
May we be so deeply rooted in Christ
that our vision is washed clean
and that we may, with Andrew,
gladly walk the way of humility and supportive love.
In Jesus' name we pray.
Amen

Bibliography

Wendy Beckett, *The Story of Painting* (DK Publishing, 1994)

Alexander Carmichael (ed.), *Carmina Gadelica* (Floris Books, 1992)

Etienne Charpentier, *How to Read the New Testament* (SCM, 1982)

Stephen Cherry, *Barefoot Disciple: Walking the Way of Passionate Humility* (Continuum, 2011)

Timothy Fry (ed.), *RB 1980: The Rule of St Benedict* (Liturgical Press, 1981)

George Herbert, *The Complete English Poems* (Penguin Classics, 2004)

Eva Heymann, *The Deeper Centre* (DLT, 2006)

Daniel Homan and Lonni Collins Pratt, *Radical Hospitality* (Wild Goose, 2007).

Thomas Keating, *Foundations for Centring Prayer and the Christian Contemplative Life* (Continuum, 2007)

C.S. Lewis, *The Lion, the Witch and the Wardrobe* (Puffin, 1959)

Barbara Mosse, *The Treasures of Darkness* (Canterbury Press, 2003)

The New Interpreter's Bible (NIB) Vols I–XII (Abingdon Press)

Anthony Phillips, *Entering into the Mind of God* (SPCK, 2002)

Corrie Ten Boom, *Tramp for the Lord* (Hodder & Stoughton, 1974)

Rowan Williams, *The Dwelling of the Light* (Canterbury Press, 2003)

Tom Wright, *John for Everyone (Vol. 2)* (SPCK, 2002)

Notes

1 Because the date of Easter is not fixed, the number of Sundays in Ordinary Time after Trinity will vary from year to year. This collection offers the maximum possible number of weeks after Trinity, and not all will be needed each year. The Last Sunday after Trinity should be used as the final week before the Sundays before Advent, whenever its date happens to fall in any given year.

2 Corrie ten Boom, *Tramp for the Lord* (Hodder & Stoughton, 1974).

3 'Immortal, invisible, God only wise' (Walter C. Smith, 1876).

4 Stephen Cherry, *Barefoot Disciple: Walking the Way of Passionate Humility* (Continuum, 2011), p. 3.

5 Gail R. O'Day, *The New Interpreter's Bible Vol. IX*, p. 703.

6 Anthony Phillips, *Entering into the Mind of God* (SPCK, 2002), p. 29.

7 *Common Worship*, Order 1, p. 167.

8 O'Day, *New Interpreter's Bible Vol. IX*, p. 798.

9 Athanasian Creed, Book of Common Prayer.

10 *Carmina Gadelica, Vol. I* (1900); www.sacred-texts.com.

11 Daniel Homan and Lonni Collins Pratt, *Radical Hospitality* (Wild Goose, 2007), p. viii.

12 Walter Brueggemann, *New Interpreter's Bible, Vol. I*, p.719.

13 Rule of St Benedict 4.39–40, p. 183.

14 He wrote about his experiences in his book *Barefoot Disciple*.

15 Luke Timothy Johnson, *The New Interpreter's Bible, Vol. XII*, p. 205.

16 William Blake, *Songs of Innocence*, 1789.

17 Tom Wright, *John for Everyone* (SPCK, 2002), p. 163.

18 Rowan Williams, *The Dwelling of the Light* (Canterbury Press, 2003), p. 3.

19 Etienne Charpentier, *How to Read the New Testament* (SCM, 1982), p. 69.

Index of Bible passages

Also from BRF

Seasons of the Spirit
One community's journey through the Christian Year

Teresa Morgan

This book is a journey through the seasons of the year and also through the high days and holy days of the Church. In the company of saints present and past, we travel from Advent Sunday to Advent Sunday, looking for the Kingdom of Heaven and reflecting on the many ways in which God's love reaches out to embrace and transform the world. Interspersing prose with poetry, this is a book to read slowly and reflectively, stilling our minds to the rhythms of grace and opening our hearts to the peace that passes all understanding.

It's wise and generous; it's accessible and full of insight; it refreshes the soul.
FROM THE FOREWORD BY JOHN PRITCHARD BISHOP OF OXFORD

ISBN 978 1 84101 710 5   £6.99
Available from your local Christian bookshop or direct from BRF: visit www.brfonline.org.uk.

Also from BRF

Time for Reflection
Meditations to use through the year

Ann Persson

It is not easy to switch from activity to stillness, from noise to silence, from achieving to letting go, from doing to being in the presence of God. This book of biblically rooted meditations provides accessible and practical routes to exploring prayer as that way of being in God's presence, letting the sediment of our lives settle so that we may have a true reflection of ourselves and of God within us.

Loosely based around the seasons of the Church year and also drawing inspiration from the seasons of nature, the meditations range from short 'spaces for grace' to longer exercises that can form the basis for a personal quiet day or retreat.

ISBN 978 1 84101 876 8   £8.99
Available from your local Christian bookshop or direct from BRF: visit www.brfonline.org.uk.

Walking with Gospel Women
Interactive Bible meditations

Fiona Stratta

Imaginative meditation can be a powerful way of attuning ourselves to God's presence, involving as it does the emotions as well as the mind. This book offers a refreshing and inspiring way into Bible study, using meditative monologues based around many of the women of the Gospels. Through a time of guided reflection, we identify with the woman concerned and see what lessons emerge for today as we ponder her story.

Each chapter consists of a monologue, linked Bible passage and discussion material designed to draw out deep communication and group fellowship, as well as trans-formational learning. While designed primarily for small groups meeting to grow their relationships with God and with each other, the monologues can also be used as a way into silent reflection either for individuals or with larger groups (for example, the monologues could be adapted to use in Sunday worship—for intercession, a time of reflection or as part of a sermon).

ISBN 978 0 85746 010 3   £7.99
Available from your local Christian bookshop or direct from BRF: visit www.brfonline.org.uk.

Simple Gifts

Blessings in disguise

Kevin Scully

We are familiar with the idea of friendship as a gift, something that bestows blessing on our lives. Hospitality enriches both giver and receiver, while humour is a gift that, used sensitively, can shed a warm light even on a bleak situation. There are other aspects of life that we may take for granted or even actively dislike—aspects such as ignorance, tears, grief, and anger.

Drawing on scripture, song, poetry and insights from daily life, Kevin Scully considers different facets of ten such gifts, from the familiar to the unexpected. He shows how each has the potential to be a source of personal wonder and joy and can also draw us closer to God and to one another. *Simple Gifts* is a book that can be read from beginning to end or dipped into for reflection or inspiration.

ISBN 978 1 84101 851 5   £7.99
Available from your local Christian bookshop or direct from BRF: visit www.brfonline.org.uk.

Also from BRF

Rhythms of Grace
Finding intimacy with God in a busy life

Tony Horsfall

Rhythms of Grace emerges from a personal exploration of contemplative spirituality. Coming from an evangelical and charismatic background, Tony Horsfall felt an increasing desire to know God more deeply. At the same time, he felt an increasing dissatisfaction with his own spiritual life, as well as concern at the number of highly qualified and gifted people involved in Christian ministry who experience burn-out.

In this book he shows how contemplative spirituality, with its emphasis on realising our identity as God's beloved children and on being rather than doing, has vital lessons for us about discovering intimacy with God. It also provides essential insights about building a ministry that is both enjoyable and sustainable.

Includes questions for reflection and action at the end of each chapter.

ISBN 978 1 84101 842 3   £7.99
Available from your local Christian bookshop or direct from BRF: visit www.brfonline.org.uk.

Also from BRF

Discovering the Spiritual Exercises of Saint Ignatius
Larry Warner

This book is an adaptation of the Spiritual Exercises of St Ignatius Loyola, to help you to embark on a life-transforming journey toward Christlikeness. For nearly 500 years, the Exercises have been a tool for spiritual formation. During those years their popularity has ebbed and flowed, but they are now experiencing something of a revival across the breadth of the Church.

This is not a book about the methods or techniques of Christian formation but one that enables you to come before God through the Gospel narratives in order to encounter Jesus afresh. If you hunger for something deeper, yearn to walk with Jesus (not just read about him), and desire to embrace more of what God is doing in and through you, then this is the book for you.

ISBN 978 1 84101 883 6   £10.99
Available from your local Christian bookshop or direct from BRF: visit www.brfonline.org.uk.

Also from BRF

Prayer
Steps to a deeper relationship

Henry French

This book is about how to embark on the path of prayer, the way that will lead you closer and closer to the heart of God if you follow it faithfully and patiently.

Grounded in scripture, each chapter is filled with wise advice, plus exercises to build confidence not only in intercession, but also meditative prayer and journal-keeping. The aim is always to show how making space for prayer is not only an essential spiritual discipline but a source of deep joy.

The book concludes with a further section of helpful ideas and suggestions to put into practice what you have learned.

Here is rich common sense for anyone wanting to pray. It's the kind of book you wish you'd come across years ago. Read it, be encouraged, be refreshed—and then read it again every so often as a reminder of how profoundly simple and life-giving prayer can be.
THE RT REVD JOHN PRITCHARD, BISHOP OF OXFORD

ISBN 978 1 84101 861 4   £6.99
Available from your local Christian bookshop or direct from BRF: visit www.brfonline.org.uk.

Also from BRF

Giving It Up
Daily Bible readings from Ash Wednesday to Easter Day

Maggi Dawn

The idea of 'giving something up for Lent' is widely known and discussed today—yet how many know that the ancient discipline of the Lenten fast had several purposes? How many of us simply abstain from some treat or other for a few weeks and fail to engage with this deeper meaning of Lent?

This book shows how Lent can be a time for exploring a different kind of 'giving up', one that can transform our lives. If we are to draw closer to God, we have to be willing to give up some of our entrenched ideas about him, in order to see him more clearly. In a series of daily studies, Maggi Dawn shows how, throughout scripture, people were radically changed by encountering the true God. If we follow their examples, we can allow the Holy Spirit to shed his light on our ideas of God that are too harsh, too small, too fragile, or too stern. Then God will graciously reveal himself to us and bring us to an Easter joy that is richer and more profound than ever before.

ISBN 978 1 84101 680 1 £7.99
Available from your local Christian bookshop or direct from BRF: visit www.brfonline.org.uk.

Also from BRF

Creative Ideas for Quiet Corners
14 visual prayer ideas for quiet moments with children

Lynn Chambers

It can be difficult to help young children find the space for personal prayer in their lives, between school and friends and church. It helps to show them that prayer doesn't just have to be for Sunday school, or when they're tucked up in bed.

Creative Ideas for Quiet Corners is designed to encourage children to find space for prayer by creating a physical prayer space in the home or at church that children can visit and enjoy. Each prayer idea uses simple but effective materials to create a quiet, reflective corner. The book also offers practical support to parents and leaders, so they can help children to move at their own pace into a sense of quietness and prayer.

Creative Ideas for Quiet Corners is ideal for children aged 6–10. It is also suitable for children's workers and can be used with special needs children. Churches who have used Godly Play may find this book useful. Equally, it can be used by adults looking for a focus for creativity and prayer.

ISBN 978 1 84101 546 0   £6.99
Available from your local Christian bookshop or direct from BRF:
visit www.brfonline.org.uk.

Enjoyed

this book?

Write a review—we'd love to hear what you think.
Email: reviews@brf.org.uk

Keep up to date—receive details of our new books as they happen.
Sign up for email news and select your interest groups at:
www.brfonline.org.uk/findoutmore/

Follow us on Twitter @brfonline

By post—to receive new title information by post (UK only), complete
the form below and post to: BRF Mailing Lists, 15 The Chambers, Vineyard,
Abingdon, Oxfordshire, OX14 3FE

Your Details
Name _____
Address_____
_____
Town/City _____   Post Code _____
Email_____

Your Interest Groups (*Please tick as appropriate)

☐ Advent/Lent
☐ Bible Reading & Study
☐ Children's Books
☐ Discipleship
☐ Leadership

☐ Messy Church
☐ Pastoral
☐ Prayer & Spirituality
☐ Resources for Children's Church
☐ Resources for Schools

Support your local bookshop
Ask about their new title information schemes.